Alyssa Mastromonaco is president, global communications strategy and talent at A+E Networks. Previously she served as assistant to the president and deputy chief of staff for operations at the White House from 2011 to 2014 and as assistant to the president and director of scheduling and advance at the White House from 2009 to 2011. She worked for Senator Obama on his campaign and in his Senate office and PAC beginning in 2005. Earlier in her career she was director of scheduling for Senator John Kerry's presidential campaign in 2004 and before that was press secretary for Congressman Rick Boucher. She is also a contributing editor at *Marie Claire*. She received a BA in political science from the University of Wisconsin–Madison in 1998.

Lauren Oyler is a writer and a contributing editor at Broadly, the women's vertical at VICE.

'*Who Thought This Was a Good Idea?* is everything we've come to know and love about Alyssa over the decade we worked with her: brilliant, funny, grounded, and inspiring. Anyone who's interested in politics – especially young people – should read this book'

> Dan Pfeiffer and Jon Favreau, former communications director and speechwriter for President Barack Obama, and hosts of *Pod Save America*

'Alyssa is a force: whip-smart, humble, and funny as hell. Her writing is as fearless as she is'

> Sophia Amoruso, founder and CEO of *Girlboss*

'Few people have had as much access and influence over national events over the last decade as Alyssa Mastromonaco. No matter how serious the crisis or hard the problem, Alyssa took care of it – with great skill and professionalism, and even greater humor. This book tells that story, of a young woman succeeding under extraordinary circumstances, and throughout it all, never taking herself too seriously'

Stephanie Cutter, former deputy campaign manager for President Barack Obama

'I've often wondered how a woman can be so many things wrapped up in one dynamic package. Alyssa is my fairy godmother: she's wise, resourceful, insanely smart, and makes me laugh in a very special way. Her stories – from the frontline of the White House to her kitchen – will entertain, inspire, and humor you for a long time to come'

Amanda de Cadenet

'A combination memoir and compendium of very good suggestions about how to get ahead – very far ahead – at an early age'   *Washington Post*

Who Thought This Was a Good Idea?

And Other Questions You
Should Have Answers to When
You Work in the White House

Alyssa Mastromonaco
with Lauren Oyler

Little, Brown

LITTLE, BROWN

First published in the United States in 2017 by Twelve, an imprint of
Grand Central Publishing
First published in Great Britain in 2017 by Little, Brown

3 5 7 9 10 8 6 4

A CIP catalogue record for this book
is available from the British Library.

ISBN 978-1-4087-1077-7

Printed and bound in Great Britain by
CPI Group (UK) Ltd, Croydon CR0 4YY

Papers used by Little, Brown are from well-managed forests
nd other responsible sources.

Little, Brown
An imprint of
Little, Brown Book Group
Carmelite House
50 Victoria Embankment
London EC4Y 0DZ

An Hachette UK Company
www.hachette.co.uk

www.littlebrown.co.uk

To Mummy, Poof, and Moosie

For letting me be me since 1976

Contents

Contents

You're Probably Wondering How I Ended Up in This Situation

When I first met Barack Obama in December 2004, I'm not sure he liked me very much. I had worked for John Kerry on and off for four years, and although the secretary of state has a reputation for being aloof, the two of us had had a very warm and close relationship, pretty much from the moment I started as an assistant in his press and scheduling office in the spring of 2000. I expected my rapport with Senator-elect Obama, who was much closer to me in age and disposition, would be similar. Plus, I was coming off the presidential campaign for the Democratic nominee. I figured Obama, who was basically unknown at the time, would be thrilled that someone with so much experience—as well as so much wit and charm and talent!—would want to come and work for him.

I was wrong; Barack Obama is tougher than that. He cared less about my credentials and more about the fact that I wasn't from Illinois. He wanted someone with a connection to his constituency, which I didn't have. I think he also wanted someone who wasn't too big for her britches, and he couldn't tell immediately how I fit into my britches. Literally or figuratively—the stress of a presidential campaign is not kind to the waistline.

But I really wanted to work for Obama. After the brutal Kerry defeat, I especially wanted to work for someone who was not going to run for president—I didn't think I could take that heartbreak twice in a lifetime—but I also thought Obama was no bullshit and so, so smart. Even then it was clear he was special.

I'd heard about the position from my friend Robert Gibbs, who had quit the Kerry campaign to work on Obama's US Senate race. One day after we lost, I was in the Kerry office, doing the very solitary, depressing work of making sure everyone's invoices had been paid before we turned the lights off for good, when a message from Gibbs popped up on my AIM: "What are you doing now?"

I said I was wrapping things up, and after that, I didn't really know.

"Do you need a job?"

Yes, I did. I had been thinking about going on to work for John Kerry's PAC, but it wasn't clear I'd get the role I wanted, deputy PAC director. Gibbs told me he was working for Barack Obama, who was really great, and that he thought I should interview to be his director of scheduling— a senior adviser. Pete Rouse, a famous and beloved figure on Capitol Hill, had just signed on as chief of staff.

I told Gibbs I would look into it, and soon after, I met with Pete (who was wearing cowboy boots and jeans). He liked me and set me up to meet Obama.

Walking into the interview, I wasn't nervous, really. If you're nervous, you seem uncertain, and I've always gone into interviews with the sense that, if it works out, that's great; if it doesn't, then it wasn't meant to be. Besides, Obama was wearing a black mock turtleneck—it put me at ease.

It was a fairly run-of-the-mill interview, with Obama at the head of the table and me across from Pete and Gibbs, going over my life and my priorities. Why would I want to work for him when I wasn't from Illinois? And since I had just come from doing what was essentially a much more intense version of the same job—with a very big staff and a lot to do—wouldn't I get bored sitting around at the Senate all day?

I didn't feel like I'd nailed it. Obama bid me farewell with a classic job interview move: "We'll be in touch." But if nothing else, I felt confident in my personality—at worst, I am "good but difficult" (and a tad sensitive), and at best I am assertive but laid-back, resilient with a righteous sense of humor. Even if I don't manage to get people to like me, I can usually persuade them that I am competent and not (too) annoying.

And that's how this story starts—with the humble goal of seeming competent and not too annoying. Like most women I know, I ultimately want to be likable and trustworthy—as well as glamorous—but it's important to take baby steps.

Though Pete later told me it had taken some persuading, Obama called and offered me the job.

* * *

I wrote a lot of this book during the 2016 Rio Olympics, and even though social media was around for 2012 and 2008, this year's Games really felt like they were taking place online. If I didn't catch an event when it was on TV, it was pretty easy to figure out what had happened by looking on Twitter. And on Twitter, the commentary was much funnier.

One of the most iconic images from this Olympics was quickly turned into a viral meme by someone with 830 followers named @a7xweeman. The photo is really crazy: In the semifinal for the men's 100-meter dash, the Jamaican sprinter Usain Bolt, the fastest man in the world, is looking over his left shoulder as he pulls away from the blurry mass of his competitors, all of whom are pretty far behind him, and he is smiling. Huge. @a7xweeman's caption for this picture was, *Record scratch* *Freeze frame* *Yup, that's me. You're probably wondering how I ended up in this situation.*

I am 5 feet 2 inches and not a sprinter, or a runner, or an athlete; I switched to Pilates in 2006, after I nearly broke my teeth falling off a treadmill. (I was BlackBerry-ing.) Nevertheless, I've often felt like this during my career: "Yup, that's me. You're probably wondering how I ended up in this situation." When you see my life on paper, it's not remotely obvious how I would end up, at age 32, working as the right-hand woman to the first African American president, sitting across from him on Air Force One heading to Afghanistan, Russia, China—or, honestly, anywhere.

As I write this, I am 40 years old, not even close to the end of my career, and I've already done more than I ever could have imagined for myself. I am a townie from Rhinebeck, New York; now, it's a posh little weekend-getaway spot that appears in hashtags and cooking shows, but when my family and I moved there it had one stoplight, our road wasn't paved, and the "chicken in a pita" at Del's Dairy Creme was the pioneering predecessor of the artisanal farm-to-table movement. I graduated from high school with about 76 other kids. I was a good(-ish) student, but I was also a big fish in a small pond. My wardrobe consisted of flannels and Grateful Dead T-shirts, and my biggest accomplishment was surviving an impeachment as student body president, followed by my mean impression of Eddie Vedder. When I got a job as a checkout girl at Kilmer's IGA Market, I was the fastest and most fastidious checker on double coupon day (do not try to pass off an expired coupon on me). I loved working the Wednesday before Thanksgiving because it put my bag-packing skills to the ultimate test.

A lot of people ask me how a public school kid from Upstate New York with no connections and no Ivy League acceptance letters, who spent more time at God Street Wine shows than in academic club meetings, ended up a few feet from the Oval Office, working as one of the youngest women ever to be a deputy chief of staff for the president of the United States. Sometimes these people are being rude, like,

How could someone like you *end up in a job like* that? Sometimes they're genuinely curious. Sometimes they want to know so they can do it, too.

I wanted to write this book to try to answer the question for everyone, but especially the last group. (The jerks are least important to me, but they can still eat it.) I have come to believe that hard work and a good attitude can get you further than you could ever dream, and unfortunately, this is a really basic lesson that doesn't come up in most career advice. It's kind of cheesy, but sometimes life is cheesy for a reason.

I also wanted to write this book because I didn't see anything like it out there. When I was trying, kind of desperately, to get a job in politics, and then when I got one, all my mentors were men. Most political memoirs are written by men—because most of the people who work in politics are men—and they're usually preoccupied with legacy: reliving the glory days, dispensing tidbits of "insider" drama, and making the writer look like he has single-handedly triumphed over adversity and evil Democrats. (Or evil Republicans—trying to make yourself look good is a nonpartisan issue.) I understand wanting to leave a legacy, but I've always tried to focus on the work first, usually knowing—except in dark moments—that my glory will come in time.

At this point, you might be feeling like, "Who is this lady and why should I care?" Fair. If you Google around, you will find me, but I'm not a household name. I was once on a list of Washington's most powerful, least famous people. A lot of jobs in politics are basically about getting shit done, and

I have had a few of them. They're not as sexy as being an actual politician, but most people—including me, for example, hi—don't have the constitution to be an actual politician. The jobs are still very important, and cool, and kind of unbelievable, as the number of state dinner bloopers I recap in this book will demonstrate.

At the end of the day, I hope you can learn from all this, including the stomach problems. I'm not interested in speaking from a place of superiority; I learn things from young and inexperienced people all the time, and I've been young and inexperienced myself. I know what it's like to be treated like you rank somewhere between a baby and a run-of-the-mill moron. I have also acted like a baby and a moron at a few points, even though I am neither. I don't expect you to know who God Street Wine is—it's a jam band that broke up, sadly, in 1999—but I think my story can make you all feel less alone, less weird, less anxious, and more confident. It all turns out OK.

. . .

One day in late October 2008, almost four years after I started working for Obama and just days before the general election, I woke up to see a forecast of snow for Chester, Pennsylvania. A panic spread throughout the campaign headquarters, and especially through the scheduling and advance department, where I was working as director. Senator Obama was slated to do an outdoor event in town later that morning, and we were all waiting to see which of us would get the dreaded email. It would come from Marvin Nicholson (Obama's trip director, and my former boyfriend of six years), Reggie Love (Obama's body person), or Gibbs (Obama's press secretary); together, they made up what we lovingly called the Road Show because they traveled with Obama everywhere he went. Sometimes, disagreements would arise between the Road Show and HQ, and duking it out with your team is never fun. In HQ we occasionally had ideas that were a little campy or aggressive, but we weren't the ones who had to answer to Obama's disappointed face when he turned to them and said, "Uh, who thought this was a good idea?"

Shortly after that happened, I would usually get an email from Marv or Reg or Gibbs relaying the question. They would know full well it was me, but it was a gentle—or passive-aggressive—way of calling me out.

Anyway, Chester, PA, 2008. The forecast was bleak, and Senator John McCain was canceling his events.

I had been working with Senator Obama long enough to know that he was not fond of the cold. (He still isn't—I mean, he's from Hawaii.) But how better to show contrast with an old and tired Senator McCain than with a spry and virile Barack Obama, so dedicated to the American public that he would endure a snowstorm to tell them about his vision for the country? Talk about leaving it all on the field! I was really into this idea. He had to keep Chester on the schedule.

I went to Plouffe—as in David, the campaign manager—and laid out the facts. There was no question about it, I told him: We were keeping Chester as is. He completely agreed. Outside, in the snow, Kenny "Town Hall" Thompson—one of our best advance leads, who was especially skilled at pulling off the greatest town hall meetings in politics—was about to execute what would become one of his most famous events, and we were not going to miss out on this opportunity because of a little precipitation.

I sent the decision to Road Show and to the advance team in Chester, who were in charge of developing and executing the event. A few minutes later, the cringeworthy but expected response from Reggie was in my in-box: "Alyssa, who thinks this is a good idea?"

We all did, but that didn't matter. As the director of scheduling and advance, I had to respond that it was my idea. It was my responsibility.

About two hours later, the event began, and we watched it on TV from the headquarters in Chicago. As our boss began to attempt a speech that would convince Pennsylvania citizens to get out and vote for him, we noticed something terrible.

"It's sideways sleeting!" Dey cried. (Dey, aka Danielle Crutchfield, was my deputy and suffered the same email traffic I did when things didn't go according to plan.)

Barack Obama was on TV being smacked in the face by sleet. So much worse than snow. Basically worst-case scenario.

We watched (in horror) as the event drew to a close, and Obama reached his hand to Reggie. As we were turning off the TV, my phone rang.

"Alyssa, it's Obama."

"Hi!" I said, with my head down on the desk, girding myself for the inevitable and deserved. "The event looked AWESOME! You heard John McCain canceled all of his events, right? He looked like a total old man!"

"Alyssa, where are you right now?"

I was not sure where he was going with this, but I knew it was somewhere bad. "My desk," I replied cautiously.

"Must be nice."

Click.

The choice to keep Chester on the schedule—my decision—was always going to result in some version of that conversation. But we all knew that slowing down in the last week of October was not an option. Besides, Obama does not hold a grudge—by the time we saw each other on Election Day this would be the last thing on his mind.

You should always be prepared to defend your choices, whether just to yourself (sometimes this is the hardest) or to your coworkers, your friends, or your family. The quickest way for people to lose confidence in your ability to ever make a decision is for you to pass the buck, shrug your shoulders, or otherwise wuss out. Learning how to become a decision maker, and how you ultimately justify your choices, can define who you are.

This decision was not dissimilar to what happened when I put Sun-In in my hair at seventh-grade field day even though my mom specifically told me not to: painful at first, but it worked out in the long run. The Chester fiasco was notable for more than just our drama. A week and change later, we had won the general election, carrying the District of Columbia and 28 states, including Pennsylvania. The next year, Damon Winter, a photographer from the *New York Times*, received a Pulitzer Prize for his coverage of the campaign, and the winning work included a photo he took of the event. Though the soon-to-be POTUS teased me for it for a little while afterward, Winter's award vindicated how everyone felt that day—including Obama. It became one of our favorite moments. The sleet pelting him in the face was front and center. And my hair is blond to this day.

* * *

I first walked through the gates of the White House about a month before Obama took office and I would officially start working there. I was going to be the assistant to the president for scheduling and advance—basically the same thing I had been doing, but like 50 times more complicated. Assistant to the president is the most coveted position in the White House; there are only about 20 to 25 of them at any one time. I was one of the youngest women to ever hold that title, if not the youngest.

Dey and I got dropped off outside Caribou Coffee and shuffled our way down Pennsylvania Avenue, both regretting the past three months; breakfast bagel sandwiches with extra meat had become the rule, not the exception. I was scared shitless. Between my physical discomfort and my anxiety, I was sort of a wreck.

We got to the gate by the Eisenhower Executive Office Building and presented our IDs, and the agent told us our meeting that day would not be in that building—instead, it would be in the West Wing. We tried to convince the guard he was wrong, but he wasn't. After we went through our security screening—eagerly handing over our IDs again and waddling through the magnetometers—we held hands all the way down the walkway, past Pebble Beach where the reporters do their stand-ups, and into West Reception. Marines opened the doors for us. We looked around and wondered if they thought we were someone else, but then we just kept walking. (Another good piece of advice is to look like you belong.)

West Reception is hard to process—it's like if the waiting room for your office were a museum. Heads of state, diplomats, celebrities, and activists all walk through it on their way to meetings in the West Wing or with the president. It was a week or so before Christmas, and all the holiday decorations were up. We chatted about the wreaths and the trees and the ornaments—they are always very beautiful—while we waited to see Josh Bolten, President Bush's chief of staff, who wanted to welcome us and see if we had any questions for him. Besides, like, "What now?"

After our meeting ended, Melissa Bennett, President Bush's director of scheduling, took us to the Oval Office. The door was open, but we were so nervous that we just stood at the threshold. We were being such tools, but we knew no other way to be. Finally, they coaxed us in.

The Oval Office was much brighter than on *The West Wing*, which was off-putting for a second; it almost looks more like a TV set than what you see on TV. (I would later learn that they keep it that way so reporters don't have to bring lights to shoot there.) The wallpaper is the best wallpaper you have ever seen; the artwork would be in a museum if it weren't in the White House; the desk is *the president's desk*. Yet everyone was so happy and friendly and kind to us. At some point, I realized I wasn't watching a TV show—this was going to be my life.

CHAPTER 1

Leadership, or Born to Run Things

The bathroom situation in the West Wing is probably not what you would expect: Toilets do not exactly abound. For women, there was only one full restroom on the ground floor, plus a single toilet in the hall on the main floor and one on the third floor. You would often find yourself waiting in line. What's more, the bathroom you were waiting in line for was not some elegantly decorated powder room with a gilded mirror and a pink fainting sofa and fancy soaps and lotions selected by Nancy Reagan and Jackie Kennedy. Besides a little primping antechamber with a countertop and a mirror, it was your standard office bathroom—three stalls, some sinks, unflattering light, and that's it.

On top of this, there were no tampons. I didn't think this was a big deal when I started working in the West Wing in 2009, but it was a huge pain to get out of the White House once you were already on the grounds—there was no running across the street to CVS between meetings. To leave, you had to brave the lines of tourists stopping in the middle of the sidewalk to take photos, and to come back, you had to show your ID, input your special code, put your bag through the security scanner, go through the metal detector. Everyone was always too busy to go through this in the middle of the day. (This is also why we always ate at the Navy Mess, the cafeteria across from the Situation Room where the Navy serves breakfast and lunch every day.) If it was a true emergency, I would sometimes ask my assistant, Clay Dumas, to run to CVS, but I started doing it so often that I began to feel guilty about it. He was busy, too.

The White House was also not a scene where you could just bum a tampon from your girlfriends. Though this is changing, there are not a ton of women working in the West Wing, and many of those who are there have already gone through menopause—not many people traveled with a stash of Tampax. Those of us who did still get our periods developed an understanding with one another, and with our assistants, that it was cool to go through someone else's bag or drawer in search of a feminine hygiene product while she was out. Still, it was not uncommon to find yourself in a... code red.

To support one another through the gender imbalance in the West Wing, some of the senior staff women and Cabinet secretaries organized regular dinners where about 15 of us would get together, talk about issues, and drink some wine. Perhaps appropriately, I got my period on the day of one of these dinners.

That workday was extremely busy, and I exhausted my tampon supply with no chance to replenish. As the time to leave for dinner approached, I began to do some calculations in my head. They weren't good. I needed to change my tampon, soon. Before I left.

I began to panic. Neither Danielle nor any of the girls downstairs had anything that could help me. The toilet paper in the bathroom was not absorbent, so you couldn't do the thing where you roll it around your underwear to make a diaper. I decided I would have to run to CVS before the dinner started.

No luck. A meeting ran long, POTUS had a question I had to find the answer to—I don't know what happened, but I ran out of time. I hopped in my car and barely made it to the dinner—I was one of the younger women going, so I didn't want to be late.

I thought everything was going to be OK, but I was wrong. In the middle of the dinner, someone said something funny, and as I began to laugh, my hearty "Ha!" quickly turned to, "Oh my God, oh my God, no no no." It was then that I began to bleed through my pants—coincidentally, also my favorite pair at the time. Blue-and-white houndstooth capris from J.Crew.

Of all the women at the table, probably about four of us still got our periods, and I knew the others didn't have tampons because I'd already asked them. I decided to abandon my dinner. I leaned over to my friend Kathy Ruemmler (who was White House counsel) and told her what was happening. She escorted me out to my car, where I bled on the front seat as I made my getaway.

The next day, I made it my mission to get a tampon dispenser in the West Wing women's bathroom. If we were truly serious about running a diverse operation and bringing more women into politics, we should give the office a basic level of comfort for them. Even if you had to pay a quarter, it would be better than menstruating all over the Oval.

There was no objection to my proposal; it just seemed like no one had thought of it before. I went to the head of the office of management and administration, Katy Kale, and said, "Hey, we should put a tampon dispenser in the women's bathroom," and she said OK.

A couple of weeks later, I walked into the 8:30 AM senior staff meeting—populated by about 20 or 25 people, including a lot of men—in the Roosevelt Room. The Roosevelt Room is a stately conference space where FDR once kept an aquarium and several mounted fish; today, it's decorated in subtle beiges, with a painting of Teddy on a horse in Rough Riders gear and a little statue of a buffalo. It was there that I announced the West Wing would be installing a tampon dispenser in the women's restroom that day. No one said a word, but it felt really good.

. . .

I realize I promised you that I didn't want to focus on "my legacy" in this book, but since they didn't engrave the tampon dispenser with "Made possible by Alyssa Mastromonaco," I wanted to leave a record of it somewhere. There are times when you need to be a bull in a china shop to get something done, and I'm capable of that, but I usually don't enjoy it. For me, leadership has always been much more about rallying people around a project or cause than about being held up as the Boss.

But leadership is not all triumph and victory; if your ideas don't work out, being a strong leader can carry you through to better times. My first formative experience with being in charge was when I was elected junior class president in high school. Even with my nuanced, enlightened approach, I was not popular. I ran for the position because I wanted to take the lead on prom planning for our senior year. (Turns out you actually only needed to be on prom committee for that, but oh well.) We ended up using the song my best friend, Cara, and I wanted, "All I Want Is You" by U2, for our special prom anthem. (I don't know why you need one, but you do.) Our theme was Riches in the Night, which is a line from "All I Want Is You," so we thought we were extremely provocative and edgy.

It almost didn't happen. After I was elected, a rival classmate decided that my junior prom date, who had a white Bronco with an eight ball tinted into the back window, was inappropriate.

The eight ball implied—but did not necessarily confirm, given how much high school boys love bragging—that he was a drug dealer, and my rival launched an impeachment campaign against me weeks before the dance. The betrayal culminated in my class adviser interviewing me about why I was a good and worthy class president in the gym in front of all my classmates, who were sitting on the bleachers.

I was furious, but I had to push forward. Senior prom could *not* be lame!

The people voted, and I remained; one of the hallmarks of a great leader is being able to explain your decisions. When I was in college and Bill Clinton was going through his impeachment proceedings, I remember thinking that not everyone could speak with the same elegance and finesse that I had displayed during Eight-Ball Gate.

Senior year, I ran for band president. Not because I wanted the glory of being band president—though it was a very high-profile position—but because I wanted our senior band trip to be to New Orleans. My platform was solid; all the members of the band agreed that we should go to the competition in NOLA. But we ended up in Philadelphia. Maybe sometimes rallying support for your ideas isn't enough; maybe taking 40 teenagers to Bourbon Street will always be a hard sell to the principal. After I left, selection of the band president became an appointed position, no longer voted upon.

᙮ ᙮ ᙮

When I graduated from college, I got a job as a paralegal for the law firm Thacher Proffitt & Wood, which was located in the World Trade Center. Initially, I was not into this; I had wanted a job on Capitol Hill, but none of the (many) places I applied hired me, so I went to a headhunter in New York City who got me an interview with TPW. (And many other law firms, but none of them called me back.) I was disappointed, but I came around. It would be exciting to work in such a famous building—I liked the hustle-and-bustle vibe immediately. Also, TPW was the only firm that didn't ask for my GPA. My grades were fine—I had a three-point-something—but at the other firms it was like you had to be Phi Beta Kappa to Xerox closing documents.

We sat in a room we called the Para Pit, and each of us worked for one partner and two or three associates. I worked for Ellen Goodwin, the only female partner, and two other lawyers. One, David Hall, took me under his wing and taught me a lot about real estate investment trusts, which still comes in handy during *Jeopardy!* or when I'm trying to convince real estate agents that they shouldn't take me for a fool.

The company had a big deal in the works—a 30-plus property cross-collateralized loan involving more than 20 states—and I was the paralegal assigned to it. By this point, my coworker Amy Volpe (rechristened "Volpes") and I were sleeping side by side in twin beds in a one-bedroom apartment in SoHo, and she would tease me about being the "Super Para" because I would talk about the deal all the time. I worked on it for months, and I got some decent attention from the lawyers about my work, but she wasn't wrong—I was so pumped that I had been given so much responsibility that it fully went to my head.

There were hundreds of documents that would need to be signed at the closing—or the sealing of the deal—and they all had multiple signatories, including notary publics. Every signatory had his or her own color—green, yellow, red, orange, blue—and because I was very thorough, I made sure to tag them all the same way so everyone could see a sea of rainbow tags when they walked into the room. This was important, because very shortly there would be about 10 people representing millions of dollars in there, and they would want to close this out fast. Each signatory was assigned a color—e.g., Chase Manhattan was green—so they could flip to their signature page, get it over with, and move on to their celebratory steak and champagne.

As the closing approached, the office started getting chaotic. Documents were being swapped out, signature pages were changing, and I was only one person monitoring it all. I was staying very late and stuffing my face with free dumplings every night. The only good thing about it was that I occasionally got to come in later, and one morning John F. Kennedy Jr. asked to borrow my newspaper while I was drinking coffee at a place in Tribeca. It was the best coffee of my life.

A real leader would have delegated and enlisted help, but few 22-year-olds are real leaders. I didn't want to share the credit with anyone else. I thought that since I had come this far and done so much work, I just needed to get it together and get it done.

On the day of the closing, it caught up with me. As all the signatories, representing tens of millions of dollars, were assembling to start signing, the notary and one of the junior partners realized something was wrong: I hadn't double-checked with the attorney on the required margin sizes (the margins of a document matter in some states). The Washington State documents were wrong. Basically useless. Couldn't be signed.

When clients pay you a bunch of money to represent them in a deal, and on the very day it's supposed to close some aspects of the closing resemble a shitshow—well, that doesn't inspire confidence. David Hall, who was effectively my boss, came up to me and very discreetly said, "Mende [that's my middle name], you are the only person who knows what is going on in this room right now, and that is scaring the shit out of me." None of the clients knew I had fucked up—and I needed to keep it that way.

I covertly grabbed all the messed-up documents and brought them to the Para Pit, in full crisis mode. We had to replace, retag, and remargin, fast. It sounds melodramatic, and it is, but at the time I was flipping out.

The other paralegals sprang into action; everyone took a set of documents and got to work. Papers were flying everywhere. I think we fixed everything within half an hour, and no one in the room—other than the notary and David Hall—knew there had been such a near disaster. Even though this was obvious before, I hadn't realized until that moment that being called the Super Para was basically the equivalent of being called a douche.

*　*　*

It was a few years later when I got a taste of how I could actually succeed as a leader. I eventually got a job in politics, with Senator John Kerry, and worked my way up to become the deputy scheduler on his 2004 presidential campaign. This meant that I came in every day, sat at my desk, talked to all the advance teams out on the road, and worked with my boss and the senior campaign staff to plan trips.

On a campaign, there is no more important commodity than the candidate's time, and when you're part of the scheduling and advance team (SkedAdv), that's what you control. This often leads to receiving a lot of enraged emails from state offices basically accusing you of ruining their chances of winning a primary or caucus because you're a dumb fuck who doesn't understand what you're doing. For example: During the Obama campaign, the South Carolina office called up this senior adviser on our team to complain about me because I wouldn't give them what they wanted; the adviser relayed their comments to me by saying, "You need to be careful before people start thinking you're a bitch."

What you realize is that everyone has her own priorities— her own constituency. Often, being a leader is not about making grand proclamations or telling people what to do; it's about balancing all these priorities and constituencies. The finance team wants time for fund-raisers. The political team wants to get meet and greets for their politicians. The press shop wants time for interviews and to make sure that the best event of the day is hitting live for the local news (this is less important in 2016 than it was in 2004, but there are still times that are better for traffic than others). The candidate wants time to sleep so they don't get too exhausted and say dumb shit. I was the arbiter of these decisions.

In the spring of 2004, my boss—the director of scheduling— got the opportunity to go back to school. I was worried about who they would hire to replace her. She was tough, but we had a very good relationship, which wasn't necessarily true with every- one on that campaign. When Mary Beth Cahill, the campaign manager, called me to her office, I prepared myself for the news. I never thought that she would offer the job to me.

But she did. I was 28.

I worked with Terry Krinvic (Tey), who had been sched- uling longer and on more campaigns than I had, and it felt weird that I was her boss. But I had been around the Kerry crew longer, which counted for something, and Tey was cool about it. Jessica Wright was our very smart assistant; she had just graduated from Wellesley, and we had her doing things like calling restaurants in the cities Kerry was going to be in so that we could get copies of their menus to order dinner for him and the team to take on the bus or plane. Glamorous and fulfilling.

As we drifted into late spring, we hired a few more schedulers, but late June bit us in the ass—we were getting ready to choose a vice president, and the convention was coming up. We had decided to do a swing into the convention—a thematic, multiday trip that would hit on key points of Kerry's biography—and then go on a tour called both Sea to Shining Sea and Believe in America, which would leave Boston the day after the senator accepted the nomination. The Kerry campaign was notorious for having too many slogans—approximately 13 by Election Day—because we could never pick just one. My favorite was "The Real Deal," which we put on a bus in Iowa that we called the Real Deal Express; there was also "A stronger America begins at home," "A safer, stronger, more secure America," "The courage to do what's right for America," "Together, we can build a stronger America," "A lifetime of service and strength," "Let America be America again," "A new team, for a new America," "Stronger at home, respected in the world," "America deserves better," "Let us make one America," "Hope is on the way!" (weirdly prophetic), and "Help is on the way!" Not only does it look ridiculous every time you change your slogan, but you also have to change the placards and banners and all the other slogan-covered things and have them shipped to you. It costs, like, $10,000.

The tour was 3,500 miles across 20 states and something like 52 cities in 17 days; it involved buses, trains, and *boats*. Having never done anything like this, or heard of anyone doing anything like this, I didn't know if my apprehension toward the plan was just me being afraid I would fail or if it was actually ludicrous. Parts of the tour were based on something Al Gore did in 2000, but it wasn't this extreme. I had misgivings from the start—if only for the fact that on campaigns you want ultimate flexibility, and the minute the train left the station (literally and figuratively), we lost that completely. But you don't want to be the "can't" person. Especially when everyone having a sense of optimism is really important.

I thought it wouldn't work, but I didn't *know* it wouldn't work, so I didn't say anything. That might be the difference between men and women: Women need to know they are right before they stand up. Men are OK objecting if they just think they might be right. I thought, but I didn't know.

The tour was, in fact, too much. We executed it, but barely, and it broke almost everyone involved. Tears, night terrors, panic attacks—you name it. Everything was harder than we expected. Two families, little kids, elected officials, time zones. The most important thing I had wanted to do was let each scheduler leave the night before their segment started in order to meet up with the traveling staff to experience what they had planned; in most cases, I had to tell them to stay behind because there was too much work to do.

From the outside, we looked smooth; the events were beautiful, we executed what we needed to execute, and the bus never broke down. But everything was constantly a photo finish, and senior campaign staff never seemed to acknowledge the stress that put on us. It was partially because there were so many senior people without clearly defined roles, and everyone else had a hard time distinguishing whose word was the final one. There were a lot of endless email chains.

One particularly awful moment was when we were trying to cut costs right before a fund-raiser in New York. At the beginning of the campaign, people had shared hotel rooms, but as the race wore on and people got fewer breaks, we started letting people have their own. Before this New York trip, every hotel was sold out; the only place we could stay was the Mandarin Oriental on Central Park. I told everyone they would be sharing rooms.

A few hours later, a young traveling assistant called me up, apparently just because she wanted to practice being passive-aggressive in a professional setting. "I heard we're sharing rooms at the Mandarin," she said. "I just wanted to know who approved that."

"I approved it. Do you want me to get confirmation from Mary Beth?"

She did. OK. I went to Mary Beth—whom I liked very much—and told her we were getting pushback about making people share rooms. (If "pushback" sounds like one of those office code words you use to say something without *really* saying it—that's because it is.) Mary Beth replied that people should always be sharing rooms.

I thought that was the end of it until some guy called me from the tarmac as he was about to board his flight to New York. "Are you fucking stupid?" he yelled into the phone. He said I reported to him, not to Mary Beth, even though I reported to Mary Beth; he was mad that I had basically outed him for spending too much money on individual hotel rooms. "Did you fucking lose your mind?"

Today, I would tell that guy to go fuck himself. But back then I was so sleep deprived, and so fed up with having no idea who was in charge, it made me cry.

By the time the Kerry and Edwards families got to Missouri—less than halfway through the Believe in America's Sea to Shining Sea tour—they were exhausted. We stopped the whole production for a day so they would not have to be physically moving, but even that was not real rest: Since we then had to push every stop back by 24 hours, we almost couldn't find hotel rooms at the last minute because the Little League World Series was in one of the towns we had planned to spend the night in. I think we ended up finding space in one of the hotels where a losing team had been staying and left early—maybe this can be some solace to them.

After the tour, I think the campaign lost some confidence in my abilities, because they brought in a "senior adviser" to oversee the scheduling and advance departments. His first move was to take my desk. We nicknamed him Bela Karolyi, after the Romanian gymnastics coach, because we felt that he treated us like little gymnasts walking to the mat for comments; he would call down the other schedulers one by one to go over their work with them. Sometimes, when he wasn't looking, we would do a little dismount pose.

I wanted to sulk, but there was so much to do that I didn't have time. I decided not to ask what he wanted my role to be and just kept doing what I had been doing. While I was hurt that they brought in someone to oversee my department, I was also 28 and had never worked on a presidential campaign before. Once he started, I think he realized that the mess of personalities I was dealing with wasn't easy. The senior team realized it eventually, too; the problems they thought the senior adviser would come in and fix persisted, because people kept making decisions too late and changing their minds at the last minute.

Campaigns always take a physical toll on you as well, but this was something else. Tey and I lived right down the street from each other on Capitol Hill, and she had a super fun Mazda Miata convertible that she would drive me home in. One day, we walked into the garage, and she realized she had left her car running for the entire workday—she was so tired when she came into work that she had just put it in park and gotten out.

A few days later, I woke up with a mouth full of blood. It hurt, a lot, but I was also very confused. After a few minutes of horrified, painful examination in the bathroom mirror, I deduced I had shattered a wisdom tooth grinding in my sleep, and the sharp edge had cut my tongue. I took Advil for a few days until I gave up and accepted that I really did have to go to a dentist.

When I went in for my appointment, he quickly assessed

that I needed all four of my wisdom teeth out immediately. That day. I said OK. He gave me a muscle relaxer and some Advil and then knocked me out. I couldn't take any time off in the middle of the campaign, so I worked from home with frozen peas on my cheeks for two days, biting down on green tea bags soaked in cold water to avoid dry socket. The peas were one of the best parts; this was late August, and it was so hot in my apartment. Besides that I just ate mushed bananas and slurred.

I wish I could say this came out of nowhere—that even at 28 I was a responsible angel who never took any risks when it came to her health—but I had experienced intense pain for weeks before my tooth broke, and I just ignored it. I knew Tey had been doing the same, so I made her go see the dentist, too. She also needed her wisdom teeth out. We were a mess.

When election night rolled around, we went off to Boston as a team. I put on my "election night" pants (read: non-yoga pants) and immediately split them with my fat campaign ass, so I had to put on my fat Gap skirt. When we all met downstairs in the hotel bar, exit polls were saying we were killing it—Kerry was up. After all that, it was such a relief. We celebrated. We drank.

And drank. And drank. As we were enjoying what was probably our one real moment of merriment, the tide turned. Ohio was looking terrible. CNN was on a TV over the bar, and it was getting weird and panicky. We all agreed we needed to go upstairs and get ourselves fresh—just in case.

Unfortunately, we were hammered. Someone puked in her purse in the elevator. Within hours of our drinking binge we were back on our computers and on a conference call, planning John Kerry's concession speech at Faneuil Hall. I guess we were lucky the space happened to be available, because I don't know where else he could have given it. But we didn't feel lucky.

The next morning in Boston was really pretty, crisp and autumnal, the way you imagine Boston, and I was trying not to cry the whole time. We all sat in a row together and listened to reporters saying really shitty things: "They ran the worst campaign"; "If John Kerry weren't so aloof, maybe he would have had a chance"; "I mean, they had SO many slogans." It was going to be four more years of George Bush. Someone from the campaign eventually turned around and told them to shut the fuck up.

When I got home to DC from Boston, I found that someone had hit my Saab, which was parked outside my apartment. She left a note with her phone number. Very nice. I called her and got a voice mail that said, "Hi! If you're getting this message, it's because I'm out celebrating four more years of George Bush! Leave me a message."

I hung up. I didn't need a new headlight that badly.

※ ※ ※

Four years later, I sat at my desk in Chicago counting down the hours to election night and reflecting on what had been a very different campaign (except for the "bitch" comment, which I survived). Our event was going to be outside in Grant Park, and the weather was freakishly good for November—75 and sunny. I fidgeted with the stuff on my desk. I checked my email. I made some lists. I was worried that it would rain during Obama's future acceptance/concession speech, and I felt like if I had a raincoat it wouldn't rain, but then I felt like it would be stupid to go and buy a raincoat in the middle of Election Day in order to ensure your candidate wins. Eventually I gave in to superstition and walked to North Face.

When I came back to the office, the whole team was gone.

I got so mad. What could they be doing? Resting on their laurels? Day drinking? How many times did I have to tell them the purse-puking story? (It WAS NOT me, I swear.) I became angrier and angrier—not that they were out, because there was nothing to do but wait, but that they were jinxing everything. In reality, they were gone for only about an hour, but if you're sitting at your desk "not looking at" exit polls, any length of time feels like eternity, and it was only 1:00 PM.

When they all came back, I was prepared to give them some really biting commentary—but then they gave me a gift: this really funny picture of me and Obama sitting on a street corner in South Carolina, with a handwritten note from him, all in a frame.

By the time evening rolled around, people had started to get on the trolleys we rented to take supporters and staff down to Grant Park—Lake Shore Drive was closed to traffic, and this was our festive idea for transportation. I kept telling the team I would catch up with them later; I thought I was going to pass out from nerves. I was the last person on my floor. Finally, Dey and my good friend Jessica Wright—Jess was also on my team—came up to me and made me leave; they weren't going to let me sit there by myself as the votes came in. It was also pretty clear that I alone could not sink the ship, regardless of what had happened four years before.

We put on the wristbands to get into Grant Park and went down to Houlihan's to pregame with some Pinot Grigio and buffalo chicken baskets. We were down to a few tenders when New Mexico was called and then, I think, Ohio. At one point, we all looked at one another and just said, "Oh my God!"

We paid our bill, ran over to the Hyatt, and got one of the last trolleys to Grant Park. Lake Shore Drive was quiet, but as we got closer we could hear people cheering and screaming. Our trolley pulled up to the VIP entrance, and we jumped off and ran as fast as we could. There he was, good old Wolf Blitzer, saying, "CNN can now predict Barack Obama will be the forty-fourth president of the United States." We got there just in time to see the reaction.

The scene was surreal. Reverend Jesse Jackson was trying to lift Oprah up so she could either see better or get over a fence. Brad Pitt was standing next to us and crying.

I stayed for a little while to celebrate, but I was home by midnight. I had to be ready for the next day.

I had relocated to Chicago for the campaign, and I lived in River North, a neighborhood not that far away from Grant Park. When I first got there, it was silent—totally surreal. I got ready for bed feeling crazy—elated yet tearful, exhausted yet wired. It was still warm out, so I opened the windows. As I set my alarm for 5:30 AM, I could hear kids coming down the street chanting, "Yes we can!"

*　*　*

I learned a lot about leadership from Obama. (Obviously.) As a boss, he isn't someone who makes you feel like you have to prove yourself; there's no external pressure to make you procrastinate or take shortcuts. He never yelled or demeaned people—even if you let him down, he would move on if you admitted it up front. He assumed we were all adults and learned our own lessons.

As a president, he could be a bit more aggressive if the occasion called for it. In December 2009, we went to the UN Climate Change Conference in Copenhagen. In the days and weeks leading up to the summit, we didn't know if POTUS would need to be there; progress on negotiations was slow, and it wasn't clear if the negotiators would be ready for heads of state to get involved.

About a week before the convention, we decided to make the trip, but on a totally crazy schedule: POTUS would get off the plane at about 7:00 AM, head over to the convention center immediately, and get out of there when negotiations were over without even staying overnight. The summit was very close to Christmas, and we didn't want to get stuck in Denmark if the weather was bad.

When we got to the convention center, the vibe was off—chaotic and tense. For one thing, they also hold the Copenhagen International Fashion Fair at the same location, and the waiting room where they kept the US delegation contained what I can only describe as an abandoned denim bar: There were a bunch of naked mannequins. For another, negotiations were not going well. Four newly industrialized countries—Brazil, South Africa, India, and China (BASIC)—formed an alliance just before the conference and committed to acting as a bloc in order to protect themselves against what they viewed as limiting measures from developed nations. It was sort of up to POTUS and the Chinese premier, Wen Jiabao, to bring everyone together on some kind of compromise.

But people were acting really weird. POTUS had requested to meet with Premier Wen, as well as with the Brazilian president, Luiz Inácio Lula da Silva; the Indian prime minister, Manmohan Singh; and the South African president, Jacob Zuma. By the afternoon, we started getting reports that the Indian delegation had left—like, gone to the airport. The whole thing threatened to unravel. The Brazilians said they didn't know if President da Silva should meet with POTUS without the Indian delegation; the South Africans said Zuma wouldn't do it without the others, either. No one knew where any of the leaders were—except for Singh, who had apparently gone home.

Suddenly, Secretary Hillary Clinton, who was heading up the negotiations with POTUS, came over to me. "Alyssa, can you confirm the Indians are at the airport?"

We sent our advance team to survey the convention center and figure out what the hell was going on. Soon, we heard that the Indian delegation were not on their way home but at a "secret" meeting called by Premier Wen. One by one, emails came in: All the missing delegations were in the same room. They wanted to avoid negotiating with us.

POTUS and Secretary Clinton didn't waste any time. They rallied a few key players and headed to the conference room where the meeting was supposedly taking place.

They arrived outside the room to find a bunch of shocked Chinese officials who tried to send them in the other direction. Gibbs got into an argument with a Chinese security agent; in the meantime, POTUS waltzed through the door and exclaimed, grinning, "Premier Wen! Are you ready for me?" Secretary Clinton wrote in her memoir that she "ducked under" the Chinese guards' arms to make it inside.

Everyone was totally flabbergasted—but then, thanks to the leadership POTUS and Secretary Clinton displayed, they were able to hammer something out.

But that was not the end of it. As the negotiations stretched longer and longer, I sat in the denim bar with the rest of the delegation and began to get reports that the weather in DC was not looking good. A snowstorm was closing in on the city, and if we didn't leave soon—like, right then, according to the military aides—they would close Andrews Air Force Base before we could touch down. The military aides began to pressure me to pull POTUS out of his meeting so we could make it home.

Even though pretty much everyone disagreed with me, I made them wait. (There also wasn't much food around, though General Jones, a national security adviser, eventually showed up with a case of wine.) The situation had been so tense—and the stakes were so high—that I knew we had to give POTUS as much time as he needed.

The meeting ended up lasting about an hour and a half, and we took off out of Copenhagen two and a half minutes before we would have been held there because of weather. Although it was the roughest landing we ever made in Air Force One, POTUS got an agreement out of that meeting. Persistence will get you far, and leaders have to champion the push.

■ ■ ●

After Obama won the election in 2008, I kept my job, as director of scheduling and advance, for the president, until I was promoted to deputy chief of staff for operations in January 2011. I got the promotion because Jim Messina decided to leave his position as deputy chief of staff to be the campaign manager for the 2012 reelection, and in a matter of hours I had been offered the job and accepted it. It was a "reach" job—not a lateral move—but there was no question about whether I wanted to do it.

I had very little time to prepare my questions for Jim, and even less time to spend with him and ask them. I got about 15 minutes to interview him and figure out how I was going to do this. "This" being: oversee all the goings-on of the White House campus; serve as the acting chief of staff for the president whenever he traveled; manage presidential events and the hiring process for the executive branch; screen nominees for Cabinet positions; and coordinate among the Secret Service, the first family, and the White House Military Office (WHMO), including Air Force One and Marine One.

My first question was: "How do you decide who gets West Wing office space?"

Jim laughed. "That's the hardest one, and it sucks." I would soon learn this myself. Besides that, he offered no counsel other than "You'll figure it out" and warning me to double-check the roster of names for any military air requests—the "manifests"—to make sure none of the Cabinet secretaries was trying to sneak friends on board. After that, I was on my own.

My assistant, Dan Brundage, helped me organize all the briefing binders the departments that reported to me had submitted so that I could brush up on things: Office of Management and Administration (which oversees the Executive Office of the President, the budget, White House personnel, and the work on the 18 acres of land surrounding the house); Presidential Personnel (responsible for the nominations and appointments of political staffers in the agencies, many of which require Senate confirmation—everything from the secretary of state, to ambassadors, to placing people on boards and commissions); and the White House Military Office. Scheduling and Advance and the Secret Service got a break, since I already knew about them.

George Mulligan oversaw the WHMO. The WHMO works with agencies like the Department of Defense to run classified construction projects and maintain the continuity of government exercises—basically, if there is a nuclear attack, or DC floods, or the president is incapacitated, what does everyone do? The WHMO has teams to fly and maintain Air Force One and Marine One; they run the process for replacing or upgrading those aircraft and do upkeep for Camp David. They manage both the nonclassified and classified operating budgets—which means the money you can know about and the money you can't—for all of the above. The military aides to the president and the presidential valets, who help with his personal needs, were also part of WHMO, as was the White House Medical Unit.

Of all the departments, I thought the WHMO would be the toughest nut to crack—it was complex, scary, and procedural, and there was no cheat sheet to understanding it. You met with WHMO in a conference room in a part of the White House that you're not really supposed to talk about, and I would often be seated with high-ranking military advisers and decorated generals. I was worried I was going to look like a complete amateur when I had my initial briefing with them. It was scheduled for the first week I was deputy chief.

Before the meeting, my assistant went through the WHMO binder and highlighted some things he thought seemed important. Then I went through it—I was trying to absorb everything before my briefing so I would look totally in control. About an hour beforehand, I realized that was not going to happen. The binder looked like a prop in a serious movie based on a John Grisham novel. It included sections on construction projects; AF1 replacement; the helicopter (HMX) replacement program, which had been stalled; the operations of the Navy Mess; and the White House Communications Agency, which is the group that runs all the telecom for the president and on campus. This binder was so big it didn't even fit in my bag.

I restrategized. I went through the binder and tabbed all the things that made the least sense to me.

When I walked into the secret room you're not supposed to talk about, they had set me up at the head of the table, and I was the only woman. Everyone was wearing a uniform; I was in a Kate Spade outfit that may have involved a shirt with hearts on it. POTUS would have gotten a particular kick out of the fact that they either called me "ma'am" or "Deputy Chief." (Luckily, he wasn't there.)

They asked where I wanted to start. I opened up my crazy-looking Post-it commercial of a binder and began with the first question, which was about the helicopter replacement program. After they gave me answers, I had more questions. I think the meeting lasted two hours.

But about 30 minutes in, I got into the groove. The questions kept coming, and so did the answers. Before I knew it, I was understanding it all.

There is no bigger compliment than being intellectually curious about what someone else spends his or her days doing—it turned out that not having the answers did me no harm. The feedback I got was that the WHMO directors all "felt good about my leadership."

CHAPTER 2

Preparedness, or The Patron Saint of Digestion

Everyone thinks that traveling with the president has got to be a sweet gig—lush service, pampering, the nicest meals. It is not. Stops in each location usually last for a day, two days, something like that—it's not exactly a vacation plus a couple of casual appointments with world leaders thrown in. Everyone is working, trying to coordinate diplomacy, and thinking about what they have to do next. You're so busy that it's not always clear when you'll get to eat—sometimes you'll go the entire day without a meal.

One of the last trips I went on with POTUS was when we went to Europe in 2014. We were gone for about a week, and we visited the Netherlands, The Hague, Belgium, and Italy, where we were making a quick detour to meet Pope Francis at the Vatican before a lunch with Prime Minister Matteo Renzi in Rome. A photo of me asleep on a couch at the EU in Brussels sums up how we felt at the time: Sometimes you crush the trip, and sometimes the trip crushes you.

The morning of the meeting with the pope, the most

exciting part of the trip, I went downstairs to the hotel restaurant to get coffee. I hadn't planned on getting food, but in
a moment of weakness, I ordered some eggs, too—I figured
I wouldn't get the chance to eat again until dinner.

Eating eggs is unfortunately not a benign act for me—I
have IBS. It mostly flares up when I'm anxious or stressed,
and traveling with POTUS, I had to learn to manage
the constant possibility of almost shitting my pants in
high-stakes situations. In a foreign country, you always want
to eat the local food—the sickest I ever got was at the Raffles
in Singapore because I ordered their take on chicken Cordon
Bleu. But I am also just not good at handling eggs.

Why did I get them? I don't know. It was a rash decision. I was coming up on my last month as deputy chief, and
I was letting my guard down. My stomach started making
noises while Ferial Govashiri—also known as Pho; she was
Obama's personal aide and my former roommate—was pin-
ning a mantilla on Susan Rice.

"Alyssa," Ferial asked, "did you eat something for breakfast?" Ferial was very familiar with my digestion issues. I
told her I'd had eggs and coffee. She looked really disappointed in me.

When we got to the Vatican, I started to sweat. If you've
never been to the Vatican before, you'll think it's lame when
I say that it feels like you're in *The Da Vinci Code*, but that's
the best nonreligious reference I have for the grandness of it
all. The paintings, the architecture—you don't have to be
Catholic to think it's incredible. It's an overwhelming place
to have an IBS attack.

President Obama was scheduled to have a private audience with Pope Francis, and senior staff were set for a semi-private audience. We walked through a series of ceremonial anterooms and then lined up in precedent order (John Kerry; Susan Rice; me; and Dan Pfeiffer, Obama's senior adviser for strategy and communications and one of my best friends) in an ornate hallway to wait for our turn.

This was the moment when I had to do some reckoning. What are my priorities? Am I going to tell someone I'm about to have diarrhea at the Vatican in hopes of getting help? Or am I going to keep quiet and potentially shit myself? Which is the least worst option? I didn't know how long Obama was going to be in there, and I didn't want to miss my chance to go in—you can't just walk into the pope's chambers late. I tried praying to the patron saint of digestion—there are actually a few who specialize against stomach pains—but I felt no relief.

I told someone. By this point in my career at the White House, most of the senior staff knew about my IBS; I once had to have Ben Rhodes, the deputy national security adviser, watch the bathroom door for me at Hamid Karzai's palace while two Afghan guards played cards and smoked on the other side of it. This kind of thing really breaks down barriers with people. When you tell someone, "Here's the thing: I might have to shit on this helicopter," and they don't shun you afterward, you have a friend for life.

The team sprang into action, but they couldn't find a bathroom in the building. I freaked; POTUS was due in soon.

Finally, a junior staff member came back with some good news and bad news from the doctor.

The good news: They had president-strength diarrhea medicine.

The bad news: There was no water anywhere.

At this point, I was vaguely aware that a sense of urgency had spread through much of the traveling staff, including most of the people who reported to me: They were all engaged in the mission to find me a glass of water so I could take the emergency medicine for my impending diarrhea. I concentrated on not shitting my pants on holy ground. After what felt like 12 or 13 hours, someone came in with a glass of water.

"Where did this glass of water come from?" I asked.

No one would say. All I know is that it was a glass of water in the Vatican, and I drank it.

You meet a lot of famous, important people while working at the White House, but meeting the pope was the first time that I really felt moved. The meeting was nothing elaborate—you walk up; shake his hand; say, "Your Holiness, it's an honor"; and then you move on—and I'm not religious. But some of my family and many of my friends are Catholics, and I was struck by the sense that meeting this person would mean so much to so many people. I felt lucky.

After that, I had to go lie down in the car. Like all our drivers, the driver was a member of the military, and I always felt very embarrassed when I had to expose my digestive weaknesses to them. (My pants were also unbuttoned.) He asked me if I was OK and if he should get the doctor; I told him no. As I flung myself over the backseat, I felt something poke me in the leg. While POTUS was meeting with the Vatican's secretary of state, I had taken, like, five packs of the blessed rosary bead souvenirs they give to people at the exit, and they were all in my pockets.

.　.　.

I have always liked the feeling of being prepared. Preparation is protection you can create for yourself; for some people, the hard part may be balancing precautions with paranoia, but in my experience, you can never be too prepared. I'm talking about everything from always carrying a weird sack of stomach aids—I personally like to have Imodium and Gas-X on hand, along with some Xanax (red wine also works but is harder to pack)—to patchouli, which has the benefit of both smelling good and calming me down. I also read every bit of information I can find on someone before I meet that person, and I always read the newspaper. If you skim the actual paper—the one that is printed and that you can hold in your hands—you hit on things you would never seek out on a website. If I went through life cramming like every day was the SATs, it would be a miserable existence, but being in control and taking a beat to think about the next five steps—about what comes next—is critical. You would be surprised what five minutes here, 15 minutes there, can do to make you feel confident and ready.

When Obama was a senator, his foreign travel logistics were handled exclusively by the Senate Committee on Foreign Relations (SFRC). Aside from getting him to O'Hare (which he usually did himself), I had no real idea what a foreign trip entailed when I got to the White House. Except for one previous kind-of-traumatizing experience.

During the campaign in 2008, we had mused about taking Obama on a foreign trip to demonstrate how beloved he was abroad, to show he could handle it, and to dispel any ideas that he did not have foreign policy prowess. But it took us so damn long to officially become the Democratic nominee (June) that I assumed we wouldn't be doing the trip. Our planning window would be so short, and I thought the campaign would want to focus all our energy on rallying the American people—the ones who could actually vote.

Oh, not so.

It was nighttime in the second week of June, and we were doing a conference call with Obama. The foreign trip was on the agenda, but I assumed the call was intended to officially drive a stake into the idea and move on. By the time I dialed into the call—a few seconds late—the discussion had already gone from a possible trip to the UK and Germany to a trip to Iraq, Jordan, Israel, Germany, France, and the UK. If the phrase "LOLZ" had existed back then, I would have texted it to everyone on the call. Instead Plouffe asked me what kind of crowd I thought we could get in Berlin, Germany. "I can tell you about crowds in Berlin, New Hampshire," I said, "but I have no idea what we could do in Germany."

Nevertheless, the trip was on.

I went to bed and woke up early. This was a situation that would need to be triaged.

The next day I assembled the SkedAdv team to deliver the news to them. Emmett, Dey, Jess, Big Liz, Astri, JoeJoe, Pho, Chaseh, Tedders, Nool, Teal, Q, Levitt, Donny, and

Little Kate the intern. I think Lesser, Lillie, and Tubman were on the phone. They would have about a month to plan a trip to six countries; it was an ungodly amount of work.

But the team was beyond stoked. Everyone started shouting ideas for things that we should be thinking about. Passports, visas, translators, hotels, volunteers, per diems, translating baggage tags! Executing a foreign trip as a presidential candidate means you're not entitled to support from the US embassies in each country. We would be doing this alone—essentially as tourists. There was no time for ego.

Everyone had his or her own discrete function. First, Denis McDonough, a senior foreign policy adviser, and Ben Rhodes, then the campaign's foreign policy speechwriter, assembled our "country captains"—foreign policy experts who helped each team navigate their country.

Peter Newell—Nool—was the director of press advance and worked on all the logistics for the press that traveled with Obama. This included things like accommodations and visas, but it also meant everything from working out where Katie Couric would do her interview with Obama in Israel to making sure the hotels we stayed at could accommodate satellite trucks for live stand-up interviews. Nool also made sure the press were well fed (a hungry press corps is bad...news) and had the right setup everywhere Obama went.

Ted "Tedders" Chiodo oversaw travel logistics and secured all our hotels and visas. We sent Tedders from Chicago to DC with a sackful of cash and 60 Jordanian visa applications to be expedited. Not a single peep from TSA.

We decided our big speech would be at an outdoor event in Berlin, and we sent my deputy, Emmett Beliveau, to Germany to scout a location.

Dey, Jess, and Lizzie Nelson would run the trip—because of the time differences between Chicago, Europe, and the Middle East, this would need to be a 24/7 operation. Since Little Kate (Kate Berner) was the youngest, she was in charge of technology (BlackBerries). Each country's advance team had an anchor member who could speak the local language.

As we were transitioning from the primary to the general election, we upgraded from renting charter planes to leasing a dedicated Boeing 757, which we had to reconfigure with better seats, including a private space for the candidate. That was my job, in addition to overseeing the execution of the trip. When I told Plouffe we would need this plane, he looked up briefly from something he was typing and said, "How much?" I told him I thought that, all in, including painting the plane with "Change You Can Believe In" and reconfiguring it back to its original formation when we were done, it would come in at around $3 million.

"Fine."

When I told him that I had gotten a deal on captain's chairs for Obama's cabin, he looked up sharply and said, "How much did that cost?"

I admit, I brought this up almost entirely for the glory. I beamed as I told him I had purchased the old chairs we bought for John Kerry's 2004 plane for about $3,000 each. That was dirt cheap. He said, "Good."

The plane was going to be delivered to Chicago about

three days before we needed to take off for the Middle East. About two days before that, they sent me a picture of the newly painted aircraft. Beautiful—except the font was wrong. Here's the thing about being a decent businessperson: When you are reasonable, savvy, and polite, you get far. I had a good relationship with the plane guys, and I didn't scream at them when I saw the wonky font. I told them nicely that they had to repaint the entire plane using the Obama-ified Gotham typeface—and fast. They did it.

Eric Lesser was in charge of luggage logistics. He was a Harvard Dem in 2007 and had former New Hampshire governor Jeanne Shaheen call me to get him a job doing anything. He flew with Obama and the entire traveling press corps and never lost a bag. Ever. During this trip, he organized luggage volunteers around the world and had our baggage tags translated into five languages. (Now he's a state senator in Massachusetts.)

A few days before the advance teams were ready to depart, I came into the campaign office and saw four big moving boxes and Little Kate on the floor, eyes wild. Kate was a junior at the University of Chicago, took the summer to intern for the campaign, and somehow ended up with us. In those boxes were about 75 BlackBerries sorted into various categories—"programmed," "advance staff," "traveling staff," etc. In 2008, our BlackBerries didn't have international capabilities, so we rented a shit ton of devices that did work abroad, and Little Kate manually programmed the entire staff's 75 numbers into every single phone.

The day before the rest of us were leaving, I had Little

Kate run training seminars for all the senior staff on how to use the phones. Never was I prouder than when I heard her chasing David Axelrod down the hallway shouting, "Axe, wait! I need to show you how to use your phone!" (After graduating, Little Kate spent several years at the White House.)

The properly painted plane arrived just in time, and it was a sight to behold.

■ ■ ■

When we landed in Jordan, I was so glad to see Pho. Pho was born in Iran; when her family fled during the Cultural Revolution, they moved from Cyprus to Germany to Minnesota and finally settled in California. Before coming to the campaign, she had been the chair of the Orange County Young Democrats. She was on the Amman advance team and would be my lifeline on so many trips to come.

It was hot as shit in Amman. We spent most of that leg of the trip in a conference room completing the planning for the next stop, Israel, which was going to be a feat. We were going from Tel Aviv to Jerusalem to Sderot, back to Jerusalem, up to Ramallah, back to Jerusalem, and then to Tel Aviv to leave. We did about 18 meetings and events in a 36-hour period. At one point, a car bomb went off a few blocks from the hotel where we were staying, and we couldn't contact a member of the advance team for a while. Scary—but he was OK.

We had a legendary advance guy leading the charge in Israel. He also did not mince words; at one point, way too late in the game, we were still negotiating whether to borrow helicopters from the Shin Bet, and he told one of our own people that if he didn't shut up he was going to "sodomize him with a vacuum cleaner." My main memory of this part of trip is learning that stress can make your gums bleed. But by most other accounts, it was very successful.

The next big hurdle was the giant event in Berlin, though I wasn't too concerned—Emmett was already in Germany (and, I would find out later, completely worn out). While Israel was the most anxiety-inducing part of this trip, Berlin was the real critical moment—if we didn't pull this off, if enough people didn't show up, if the setup outside the Victory Column looked bad, we would seem like idiots.

Rolling into Berlin, we heard reports that 100,000 people were waiting for Obama. We didn't believe them, but it was true. Aerial shots of the crowd are insane: a sea of people, on tiptoe with cameras, trying to get a glimpse of the real Barack Obama beyond the series of giant TV screens broadcasting him to those in the back.

I stood with Axe, Gibbs, and Susan Rice in the buffer zone behind the stage as Obama delivered a sweeping speech about how Berlin represents the importance of international cooperation (and, subtly, about how he could be an antidote to eight years of George Bush). I'd heard Obama give countless speeches, and he has always been a brilliant orator, but this one made me so proud; we knew Barack Obama was great, but to see all these people from other countries recognize it was moving. The event was so good that John McCain used clips of it for his "Celebrity" ad, where he compared Obama to Britney Spears and Paris Hilton.

Afterward, everyone had talked a big game about going out. We were staying at the Hotel Adlon (where Michael Jackson dangled his son over his room's balcony) across from the Brandenburg Gate; I went to my room, ordered a steak and wine, and passed out by 9:00 PM. The next morning, Marv got up at 8:00 AM to help me hunt for an *apfelstrudel*, which is something my Oma, who was from Germany, used to make for me. The one we found wasn't as good as hers, but it was one of the best parts of the trip.

The jaunts through France and the United Kingdom went without incident, and I slept from London to Chicago without waking up once.

The trip was a very risky move. Taking a candidate out of the country four months before a general election can backfire in countless ways—in 2012, Mitt Romney's own trip to London, Warsaw, and Israel was deemed a "Gaffepalooza" by the *Washington Post*; the UK tabloid the *Sun* called him "Mitt the Twit." We pulled it off because we were prepared for anything that could go wrong—from massive security failures down to baggage tags.

* * *

In late March 2009, President Obama decided to make his first trip to Iraq as president of the United States. As the director of scheduling and advance, I was head of the coordinating body—we worked with the national security staff, the White House military office, the Secret Service, and the White House staff—that was in charge of figuring out how exactly this would go down.

When you send the president, or any distinguished visitor (DV), to a foreign country, it's no light matter. I'm sure you remember seeing news break one morning about the president, vice president, or secretary of state having landed in Iraq or Afghanistan. In most cases, the president flies overnight so he can avoid anyone knowing he's left the building, arriving as America wakes up so people with potentially dangerous motives don't have time to plan anything extraordinary.

It takes a lot to pull it off—you need to be able to fully trust your team to tackle the required choreography to get roughly 40 people (staff, Secret Service, press) into the air without anyone seeing. I thought that because we'd orchestrated the giant campaign trip the year before, we would be fine. This was not the case.

In 2009, we decided that, since it was our first time going to Iraq, we should make it as hard as humanly possible on ourselves. We would jump to Iraq after we finished a stop in Turkey on a previously planned OCONUS (Outside the Continental United States) trip.

In order to scoot out of Turkey and into Iraq with POTUS and a handful of staff, we pretended the backup plane (when you travel abroad, you always take two, in case one breaks) was broken, so we left without it and went off "back to DC." This means that we lied to our own staff—we kept all the people who weren't essential to staffing Obama on the ground in Turkey for a few hours, until we arrived in Iraq— and to the reporters who weren't in our press pool. We gave the White House press corps—a group of 13 or so reporters who rotate in traveling with the president—a heads-up to include them in the planning process (and to give them the opportunity to go home if they didn't want to head into a war zone), but it was under embargo, meaning they couldn't report on it or discuss it.

We were a couple of hours into the flight to Iraq when Emmett—who remained my deputy and became the director of advance in the White House after the campaign—called Air Force One to let us know a sandstorm was kicking up outside Baghdad. The thing about sandstorms is that they make it very hard to fly helicopters. Our plan had been to land at Camp Victory, our US base outside Baghdad, dash over to the helos, and take off as fast as we could for the Green Zone and our meetings with President Jalal Talabani and Prime Minister Nouri al-Maliki. We needed to figure out what the hell we were doing instead, and fast—you don't dillydally with a POTUS in Iraq.

As we huddled around the conference room table on AF1, Gibbs asked me what I had in my pockets. "Hmm," I replied, pretending to root around in there. "Nothing?" He gave me a side eye, but we were in the middle of a phone call with General Raymond Odierno, who at the time was Commanding General, Multi-National Force, Iraq, to figure out a plan B for when we landed.

Truthfully, I hadn't given much thought to what I'd brought in my pockets, but there was something in there. I had never been on a helicopter before, and I was pretty convinced I was going to puke once we got in the air. I was the most senior woman on the trip (in a sea of dudes), and I didn't want to embarrass myself (and the entire gender), so I went to Whole Foods before we left and stocked up on plastic produce bags. I carried them with me, stuffed into the pockets of my trench (I thought it had a Carmen Sandiego vibe) as a precaution. Instead of going with one or two bags, which would have been a reasonable amount of preparation, I probably had five or six and gave myself away. I looked like a college student trying to sneak cereal out of the dining hall.

The sandstorm was quite bad—but I never saw it, because we ended up landing at Camp Victory and taking the motorcade, a line of black Suburbans and two or three white passenger vans. As I took off my jacket, I came clean to Gibbs and Axe, because a lie would definitely have been weirder than the truth. I explained that I was absolutely not going to be the woman who barfed on a military commander in Iraq, and they appreciated it.

We arrived to greet the troops at the palace that used to belong to Saddam Hussein's mother-in-law. So many surreal things happened. I don't like to characterize someone's feelings about a situation, but I can say with some certainty that Gibbs was taken aback, and humbled, when the troops recognized and cheered for him. It hadn't occurred to him that they would routinely watch the daily White House press briefings he gave.

Rhodes and I sat on this really gaudy bench and waited. Then we hustled over to the general's house, where the president had his meeting with other Iraqi leaders. We ended up having to do phone calls instead of meetings with President Talabani and Prime Minister al-Maliki.

It's common to keep your phones off when you're traveling to a war zone, so no one can track your signal, but once the meetings were under way and the press had reported that Obama was in Iraq, I could use my phone again, so I called my sister. She answered the phone at work. "Oh my God, sis," she said. "Are you in IRAQ?"

We had only been in office for about two months, and I was feeling pretty cool. Although I didn't end up puking on a helicopter, preparing for that worst-case scenario allowed me to focus on the "normal" concerns of my job. Knowing that if I puked, I would have been able to do so gracefully made the whole thing markedly less stressful.

A BRIEF INTERLUDE FOR SOME MORE PREPAREDNESS TIPS

A question women often ask one another is: "What do you do?" It may refer to a skin-care or exercise regimen, or a set of dietary restrictions, or how you manage to get out of the office with zero emails in your in-box, but I think the question—which basically boils down to "How do you live your life?"—is rarely posed out of nosiness. Maybe it's genuine curiosity (which is different from nosiness). Maybe it's the compulsion to make sure that you yourself are on the right track. (Am I right to hate myself for waking up late?) Maybe there's a little desire to steal some aspect of someone else's routine for your own life. (How can I stop hating myself for waking up late?) Regardless, the answer is rarely uninteresting, even if it's totally boring. Here's what I do to stay prepared.

(1) **I always keep a list.** I love a good list. I separate it into three parts: immediate goals, long-term goals, and personal. The immediate category usually includes things like paying bills, buying cat food, making a hair appointment, or picking up a prescription. The long-term list would include things like figuring out how to register my company in New York State, paying off my car (I did it!), planning a vacation, and getting tickets for an upcoming concert. The personal is basically just a list of friends whom, during the business of my life, I don't want to forget to call, get drinks with, or

track down to get our nails done. Something like "write this book" would end up falling in all three categories and listed three times so that I would maybe get the message.

Here is a sample list from today (August 15, 2016):

IMMEDIATE:
Finish chapter 6 with LO edits
Pay Q3 tax bill (need to find envelope/must drop in Rhinebeck at dinner)
Go to PetSmart (need litter and more food for Petey)
Cut BunBun's nails
Shower
430P call with Hope
Get train tix for this week
Put trash out
Leave by 515P for din with Mom and Poof

LONG-TERM:
Update chapters 1, 3, 6 with LO edits
Write chapters 4, 5
Email Souza about photos
Lock down Sept house for LO
Make list of improvements to Germantown house
See land in Germantown
Figure out Poof b'day present
Make hair appt
Get car washed
Try valerian root

Make Petey annual vet appt
Check to see if Ace+Jig coat has shipped
Check to see if No 6 clogs have shipped
Email Molly about CORA in Target
Connect with Sophie Walker

PERSONAL:
Book shit
Read *The Girls*
Less carbs

(2) **I put everything in my calendar.** It takes so much stress out of my life to know where I can find things. My credit score went up 100 points when I started putting in reminders to pay my bills. I put birthdays in my calendar and set a three-day reminder in advance so I can put a card in the mail. (I keep birthday and all-purpose cards in the house at all times. And stamps. You should always have stamps.) I schedule reminders to pick up prescriptions or to make a dinner reservation at some bullshit hard-to-get-into place where you need to book a table 30 days out. Same for hair and gynecologist appointments—anything hard to schedule. I put my grocery list in my calendar. I almost always need 2% milk, Wheaties, watermelon, coffee, Coffeemate (don't judge), and grapefruit juice, so I keep the list to remind me in case I happen to find myself at the store.

(3) **Sleeping is good.** For a long time, I was skeptical about those thousands of books that talk about the

importance of sleep. When I worked at the White House, I started off going to bed at around 11:00 PM and waking up at around 5:15 AM, and because "going to bed" is different than sleeping, I probably slept only three to four hours a night. It was really after I turned 35 that sleep started having the greatest impact on my life, but keep it on your radar—you eat less, look younger, have a better attitude, and make better decisions if you get enough sleep. After I left the White House, even though by the end I was on a strict sleeping regimen (more on this later), I was finally able to sleep in a meaningful way, and it changed my life.

(4) **On traveling:** No matter what I'm doing or where I'm going, I try to give myself as much time as possible to get there. (I am partially motivated to do this because I get stomach cramps or diarrhea when I cut anything too close.) If making an impression is important, I fly or take a train or drive the night before.

I also learned the importance of packing from Dey. When you're working in the White House, you can traverse three distinct climates over the course of a trip, so packing is vitally important. On one trip, we started in Saudi Arabia, went to Egypt, stopped in Germany, and finally ended up in France. You will never go wrong with lots of layers and always covering your shoulders.

Because no one working in the White House had time to run around our apartments screaming, "Did I forget anything?" Dey had a packing checklist that quickly became legendary; after a year or so, we all used it religiously. Compression socks and a Snuggie (yes) for long flights. Granola bars for

places with dodgy food. Tide pens. Bobby pins for countries
with lots of humidity. Culturally appropriate footwear
and dresses for state dinners in foreign countries. Once I
accidentally packed a pair of peep-toe shoes on AF1 when
we were heading to Saudi Arabia, and everyone made fun
of me because I was afraid I would cause an international
incident when meeting the king. (You're not supposed to
expose your feet.) It wasn't the end of the world, but it
wasn't awesome. After being introduced to the packing list,
I endured far fewer mishaps.

Also, I never have fewer than two tampons in my bag—
one for me, one for a friend.

(5) **On studying:** The first lady was particularly adamant
about state dinners: They were not just a fancy spread with
free food and nice booze; they were work, and you were
supposed to show up. Part of knowing how to be prepared
comes from being self-aware—being able to anticipate what
you'll need (or screw up) and planning accordingly. I know
I am rarely, if ever, the smartest person in the room. And
that's totally OK. What's not OK is (1) not recognizing that
and (2) not coming ready to participate in a meaningful way.

At state dinners, this meant knowing who you were sitting
next to and reading up on a few things to talk to them about.
Sometimes, this is awkward; at a state dinner for China, I
was next to the commerce secretary, and although I'd looked
him up online, there wasn't a lot of information available.
Finally, I dipped into my well of go-to conversation starters,
and since there was a musical performance at this dinner, I
asked him what his favorite American song was.

Dey's Packing Checklist

	Home Checklist
	Clean bathroom
	Clean kitchen
	Clean bedroom
	Clean living room
	Email flight confirmations to AM
	Before Leaving
	Yellow card updated with shots
	Credit cards
	Charge camera
	Purchase Ziploc bags
	Withdraw cash
	Medication
	Band-Aids
	Pain reliever/Advil
	Allergy medicine
	Bug spray
	Sunscreen
	Personal hygiene items
	Toiletries
	Hair ties and bands
	Comb and brush
	Toothbrush (and the case)
	Toothpaste
	Dental floss
	Shampoo
	Conditioner
	Protective UV
	Mouthwash
	Frizz Ease Hair Serum
	Hair wrap
	Flat iron

	Curling iron
	Shower cap
	Dove soap
	Soap holder
	Razor
	Face cleanser
	Makeup remover
	Cotton pads
	Makeup
	Concealer
	Urban Decay Potion #9
	Photo finish
	Eyeliner
	Mascara
	Eyelash curler
	Eyebrow brush
	Eyebrow shadow
	Neutral shadows
	Powder
	Powder brush
	Pink Bobbi Brown blush
	NARS bronzer
	Silver lip gloss and neutral bronzer
	Tweezers
	False eyelashes
	Other Clothes
	Nike Dri-Fit pants
	Black-and-white workout pants
	2 workout tank tops
	Gray sweatpants
	1 tank top to sleep in
	1 pair of shorts
	7 pairs of socks
	Black sports bra
	White sports bra

	Tennis shoes
	Hoodie
	Eletronics
	Camera
	Camera battery charger
	2 BB chargers
	BB charger converters
	iPod
	iPod charger
	Computer
	Computer power cord
	Secure ID
	Hard pin
	Miscellaneous
	Evian
	Passport
	Pre-advance schedule
	Culture memo
	POTUS schedule
	Nap socks
	Nap neck pillow
	Sunglasses
	Umbrella
	WH badge
	WH fliptop badge
	Jewelry
	December Trip
	Sleeping bag
	Watch
	Big North Face
	Skinny North Face
	Nike hoodie
	REI pants
	Mattress pad
	Draft schedule

He said it was "We Are the World," so we spent the rest of the dinner trying to name all the musicians who sang on "We Are the World." Long after we had given up, and he was talking to someone else, he looked back and me and shouted, "We forgot Cyndi Lauper!" Everyone was very confused.

If you don't see yourself attending black-tie events with foreign dignitaries any time soon—though you never know—you can still take this advice to a job interview. When I've had to prepare for a job interview, I make sure to keep up on any news or current events related to the person or organization I'm meeting with. I read up, if I can, on my interviewer. It's entirely possible someone who interviews you might not have Google results or be on Twitter, but if they are, you should know. At the very least, company websites usually have employee bios. The person will understand if you aren't deeply acquainted with her stance on *Bachelor in Paradise*, but knowing her position in the company, how long she's been there, and maybe even where she went to college (good for small talk) demonstrate a solid effort. Don't go overboard in some psycho Instagram deep dive and open with "So I see your dog Chunk likes to eat rabbits," or "You really enjoy Pilates!"—that would put you in the running for mayor of Creeptown. But if this person has a more public profile, scan a few articles about her. One of the best/worst/most revealing job reviews I ever conducted was when, 10 or 15 minutes into the discussion, the woman stopped in the middle of what she was saying to exclaim, "Oh, waiiiiiiiit—weren't you an Obama staffer for a while?"

I never started doing the type of work I do to become famous. But part of why preparedness is so important is that everyone knows you're supposed to come to professional conversations with a couple of questions and a sense of whom you're talking to. Everyone knows how easy it is to Google. The woman I was interviewing wasn't living in a commune in the forest with no Internet access. Not knowing who I was didn't make her look like an independent spirit or focused on her own work—it just made her look bad.

* * *

We have advance teams in politics because it's often much easier—and more effective—to negotiate in person than over the phone or via email, and there were times during my reign as director of scheduling and advance or deputy chief when, because a certain trip was especially complicated, I thought it would be best for the operation if I traveled ahead of the president. One of these times was in 2011, when we went to London.

The president was going to the UK to kick off the year-long Diamond Jubilee celebration of Queen Elizabeth II—the 60th anniversary of Her Majesty's accession to the throne—and our trip had many different pieces: a dinner at Buckingham Palace; a dinner at Winfield House, the US ambassador to the Court of St James's residence, that the US was throwing in honor of the queen; and an address to Parliament, to name a few. We were sending an entire US delegation—Caroline Kennedy (who later became the US ambassador to Japan) and her husband; Tom Hanks and Rita Wilson; Brian Roberts, the chairman and CEO of Comcast; and Doris Kearns Goodwin. We wanted a group of dynamic Americans the queen might enjoy meeting. When we learned the queen liked Broadway musicals, we also invited Kristin Chenoweth to perform at Winfield House. I needed to go early to make sure every detail was sorted. It probably would have been fine if our regular advance team had gone, but I was leaving nothing to chance.

Right when we were about to start sending people off, the Grímsvötn, a very active volcano in Iceland, erupted, creating a giant plume of ash that caused a significant disruption in air travel. Planes had to avoid it at all costs—the ash was so hot it could melt engines—and it was making it very hard for our delegation to get to London. In the week before we were scheduled to depart, Caroline and I were going back and forth over email and trading calls—just a little plume talk between girls. Her son Jack's high school graduation was the weekend after the trip; she decided she just couldn't chance not making it back.

Yikes. I was hoping all the others would make it, because you really don't want poor attendance for the queen. POTUS trusted us with all these details, and the last thing you want is the dreaded Questionable Eyebrow—the one that says, "What the fuck is going on?"

As the delegation started to trickle in, the cold I'd been suffering from at the time morphed into a full-body flu. Right before the dinner at Winfield House, I left the hotel to get a blowout because (1) obviously, and (2) I had the flu and looked like it. POTUS and FLOTUS arrived in London and the trip was under way. As I finished getting ready in my room, Dey and Pho came by for some pregame prep. You can always leave it to them to say, "Um, more blush." I took two British DayQuil and went down to load the vans and head to Winfield House.

Here is where I have to make a confession: I love the royal family, and I really, really love the queen. The photos of Her Majesty driving her Range Rover with the dogs and her hat and her bag—is there anything better? I spent many weeks leading up to the trip telling anyone and everyone, including POTUS, about how my Oma would get all the German rags when I was a kid so we could read about the royals—in German, which was fine, because I was only in it for the pictures. I appreciate eye-rolling about tabloids, and even about the monarchy, but there is just something about royals. So much history and tradition, and it seems like it all comes from a time that's quickly passing by. Also, I love tiaras.

When we arrived at Winfield House, everyone looked so rad. We always saw one another in the same boring pencil skirts and cardigans from J.Crew, so the chance to don formal wear was fun when it came around. I was crushing a blush Badgley Mischka (partially because of the flu weight loss). I got all my black-tie dresses from a consignment shop in Georgetown, Ella-Rue, and they would call me when a certain similarly sized woman—size 8 plus butt—would bring in a pile of Oscar de la Rentas or Valentinos. I always sold them back afterward, at only a small loss.

Somehow, I didn't realize I was actually going to get to

meet the queen. When we pulled up to Winfield House and joined a receiving line, I began talking a lot—chalk it up to cold medicine and a quick champagne, or genuine nerves—and I only really remember Pfeiffer saying, "It's going to be OK, buddy," which was his way of chilling me out.

Queen Elizabeth II was magical—wearing a fantastic, sparkly, beaded dress and her tiara—and SO friendly. (She said "Hello.") With POTUS and FLOTUS standing next to her, looking just incredible themselves, I absolutely could not hide my glee. POTUS was looking at me like, "Please don't knock her down!" and I did not knock her down.

After that, Valerie Jarrett (VJ) introduced me to Colin Firth and his wife, Livia, a stunning Italian eco-fashion activist, and I knocked back another glass of champagne. I suddenly felt very short and cream puffy; Livia was basically a goddess. She's quite tall (to me, anyway) and was wearing emerald green. *The King's Speech* had come out pretty recently, and everyone was gushing to Firth about it. I was sort of silent—not really for any particular reason, except maybe the flu and being completely overwhelmed. Still, our job as diplomats is to entertain and engage our hosts, and I was being a dud.

At some point, probably because she is as gracious and inclusive as she is beautiful, Livia turned to me and asked, basically, "What's your favorite movie?"

Because I was out of my element and into the cold meds and champagne, I could not tell if she meant, "What's your favorite movie in life?" or "What's your favorite movie starring Colin Firth?"

(Sidebar: I highly recommend coming up with a more

or less real but small-talk-appropriate list of favorite movies, television shows, books, and music for important but irrelevant party chat like this—there's no reason a pleasantry should turn you into a sputtering idiot who apparently hasn't seen a single film. My list: *St. Elmo's Fire*, sports movies like *Miracle*, and *The September Issue*; *The West Wing*, *The Affair* on Showtime, and *The Facts of Life*; *The Perfect Storm*, because I love the descriptions of weather patterns; and the Grateful Dead, Barbra Streisand, Bruce Springsteen, and Lilith-Fair-type bands like the Indigo Girls. Done.)

I assumed she meant Colin Firth movies. I launched into a dramatic reenactment of my favorite scene from *Love Actually*, not only in front of the spouse of one of its stars but also in front of Nigella Lawson, Tom Hanks, and, most important, my coworkers, whom I would have to face in the morning. "We love Uncle Jamie! We hate Uncle Jamie!" I cried, in my best British accent. (Which is not a good British accent at all.) Out of the corner of my eye I saw David Beckham laughing. He thought I was either funny or drunk; I later told everyone I was sure he wanted to do it with me. Sorry, Posh.

We went back to the hotel and had a cocktail at the bar, where I continued to (painfully) regale Pfeiffer, Favs (Jon Favreau, Obama's chief speechwriter), and Plouffe with stories of David Beckham wanting to do it with me. Finally tired of that—and with the combination of fancy booze and British pharmaceuticals going to my head—I went upstairs, threw my shit in a suitcase, and went to bed.

The next morning, I got a knock on the door from Reggie Love. "Boss wants you on Marine One today."

In other words, POTUS was requesting that, instead of going ahead with the staff in vans to Stansted, I head over to Buckingham Palace to say good-bye to the queen with him and the first lady and then depart with them on Marine One, the helicopter that transports POTUS and FLOTUS to the airport.

This was a problem.

When you travel with POTUS and you are leaving on Air Force One in the morning, you usually put your luggage outside your room the night before so it can be loaded onto the plane in time for departure. Seeing as I was just planning on riding in the staff vans to the airport in advance of POTUS and FLOTUS, who were scheduled to visit Buckingham Palace before meeting us all at the airport, and I still wasn't feeling that great, I had left out a brown tweed blazer (thank God), a sweater, and jeans for the next day. Jeans and more casual clothes were generally acceptable if no one (read: the press corps or foreign diplomats) was going to see you. POTUS and FLOTUS didn't really care if you wore jeans on the plane.

But Barack Obama—a truly sneaky dude. He knew I was dying to see Buckingham Palace, and he had succeeded in surprising me with the opportunity to do so. He knew I hadn't attended the dinner held there on the first night of the trip and how much it would probably mean to me to be able to see the palace in person. He had kicked someone off Marine One so that I would have a reason to go.

So: There I stood, in my jeans and sweater and flats (at least I didn't have my Birks on), looking at Reg with horror in my tired, slightly hungover, still a little flu-ish eyes, the weight of this amazing gesture pressing down on me. "I'm not dressed," I said. "I can't go to Buckingham Palace."

He replied, simply, "You think I'm telling POTUS that?"

I grabbed my big leather bag (and source of my back problems) and got in the Suburban to roll over to Buckingham, popping two Imodiums to preempt my nervous stomach. We walked into the palace, and while POTUS and FLOTUS said good-bye to the queen, I made a beeline for the drawing room, where there was a safe space behind the couch. I fidgeted, pretended to read a magazine, and prayed the staff would not notice what a rube I was.

Finally, everyone started to make motions like we were getting ready to leave; I could barely take in the place because I was so freaked out. I cozied up to one of the president's valets, who had some of his bags, and begged to carry one. No way. So I just moved very close to a suitcase and shuffled across the grand lawn and over to Marine One, which was waiting for us.

I took a second to look back, and what a sight. Prince Philip and the queen were saying good-bye, and the entire house staff was lined up on the lawn to wave to POTUS and FLOTUS.

When we were loaded up and lifting off, I breathed a sigh of relief. No one had noticed my outfit!

Then POTUS turned to me, looked down, and said, "Jeans?"

"I'm sorry!" I replied. "I didn't know!"

He looked me up and down again. "*What* is that?"

It was the issue of *Tatler* magazine that I had accidentally stolen from Buckingham Palace when I was too preoccupied with hustling out to the helicopter to remember to put it back.

    ■ ■ ■

I learned some important lessons that day. The first: When you are within 10 miles of the queen, carry a damn pair of trousers on your person at all times. The second: Unless you're going to the Iowa State Fair, always hedge on the side of more professional.

I didn't get a Buckingham Palace selfie—I was tweaking out too much to think of it, though I have no idea if that would have been allowed. (Another tenet of preparedness is to always know the rules beforehand, even if you want to break them.) But I did, at least, get a souvenir out of the whole thing. That issue of *Tatler* is in a box somewhere in Manhattan Mini Storage. I'm pretty sure Lily Collins was on the cover.

CHAPTER 3

Independence, or You Can't Just Tagalong

In 1994, the Republicans decided they were going to win back Congress, and to do it they began a campaign that came to be known as the Republican Revolution. The Republican Revolution was designed to unite the party and provide an alternative to Bill Clinton. Written by Newt Gingrich, the House Minority Whip, and another guy, Dick Armey, with some flair from Ronald Reagan's 1985 State of the Union address thrown in, the revolution's manifesto was known as the Contract with America, and it outlined what the party would do if they won the majority in the House of Representatives during that year's election. What they would do: Create or uphold systemic obstacles for the lower classes, women, and minorities, mainly. (They made their intentions very clear—the Contract's welfare reform plan was called the Personal Responsibility Act. There was also a Family Reinforcement Act and a crackdown on crime.) Newt went on a tour of the United States to promote it.

At the time I was an 18-year-old freshman at the University of Vermont, and although my family wasn't super political, I had felt the excitement of the 1992 election and even thought about going to Bill Clinton's inauguration, though I was ultimately too scared to make the trip to DC. More important, I was extremely impressionable. I was raised to think and act for myself, but I still often did things because all my friends were doing them—not to be cool, really, but because I was curious and wanted to try. So when it was announced that Newt would be visiting Burlington as part of the Contract for America campaign, and a group of people from my dorm said they were going to protest, I was like, sweet, I'm there.

The University of Vermont has a reputation for being liberal, and of course the state produced Bernie Sanders, but in general it's not exactly like socialists are hanging from the rafters. About a hundred people had come to hear Newt speak. We showed up downtown outside the place where the event was being held and waited to make our move.

After the event ended and Newt was in his car and trying to leave, we pushed forward, yelling and chanting and shaking our fists. As his car was moving slowly through the crowd, I got caught up in it, and then I did what felt natural: I jumped on the hood.

It was totally exhilarating, despite my previous ambivalence. There I was, a lowly freshman, making a political impact on top of the despicable Newt Gingrich's chauffeured vehicle. I was only there for a couple of seconds before rolling off and letting someone else have his turn. I felt like the coolest person in the world.

Unfortunately, a bunch of liberal college students hopping on the roof of a car had little effect on the Contract with America campaign. The Republicans won 54 seats in the House, giving them the majority for the first time in 40 years, and nine Senate seats. The next year, Newt became the Speaker of the House and *Time* magazine's Man of the Year.

Still, I was hooked. It probably helped that I didn't get in any kind of trouble for doing it—all in all, it was a pretty low-stakes protest—but maybe that was a blessing. It made it feel easy—and fun—to get involved in politics, and I couldn't wait to do something like that again.

* * *

I recognize that many people would not just fling themselves onto a controversial politician's car in front of a bunch of people they were trying to impress, but I have always just kind of gone for things. I am stoked—and lucky—that I was born in the '70s. If I could have picked any other time to be born, it probably would have been the early '60s, so that I could have toured with the Grateful Dead in 1978. That summer, the Grateful Dead played Red Rocks Amphitheatre outside Denver, and it was said (and I agree) that they "elevat[ed] the Red Rocks beyond their already spiritual planes." I loved listening to those shows.

That said, I wouldn't want to stray too far from my actual generation. In the '70s, people were still chill. I don't want to be too nostalgic, especially because the present day has a lot of benefits—women's rights, Google Maps—but I think the idea that times were simpler "back in the day" is true in a lot of ways. Whatever anyone tells you about how technology and social media have made us disconnected from reality is probably right, but I think you can boil all these kinds of arguments down to the fact that people are no longer chill. They are goal-oriented. They are aware of all the things they could or believe they should have. They are aware of all the things that could go wrong. This awareness makes a lot of things—dating, finding a job, dating a person you meet at your job, planning a trip for the president of the United States—much harder.

My parents were 26 when I was born—1976—and I just remember them rolling with life. Memories are faulty, sure, but my mom and pop tell stories about going out when they were dating, and it just sounds so *nice*. They would eat Chinese takeout and watch *All in the Family* and *M*A*S*H* and take Opie's car to get gas during the 1973 oil crisis. See? Simple. Pleasant. Fun. You ate what you were given. There were no designer menus. There was no worrying about whether your kale or your tampons were organic. My dad used to let me help make meatballs—two years old and just crushing some raw meat with my bare hands. I'm not sure how many parents would let their kids do that now, but it was so fun, and I survived. There are more than a few photos of me sneaking the last sip out of a beer bottle.

I don't want to give you a "when I was your age" speech— I like organic kale, I invest in an organic tampon company because I believe they truly are life-changing, and I often order lunch through Seamless, which is maybe the complete opposite of "You ate what you were given." Today, we have many more choices, and while these choices allow us a freedom I could never have imagined growing up in tiny Rhinebeck, they also make it easier to veer off course.

To be fair, I had a lot going for me. Until my sister was born, I was the only granddaughter on either side of my family, and I got a lot of attention. But I don't remember seeing things other people had and wanting them. I remember specific moments when I just felt content, and I still am. I think that even at a young age, I had a sense that life was what you make of it. That, and the confidence that jelly donuts are about the best thing on Earth. The two things are probably related; if a $1 jelly donut makes you really, really happy, you can get through a lot with a little.

If I'd had parents whose goal for me was to be successful—to be a doctor or a lawyer or a CEO—I probably never would have ended up where I did. It's also safe to say that if I had woken up one day during high school and said, "Mom, I figured it out. I want to be deputy chief of staff for the president! I think I can swing it by the time I turn thirty-five. What's for dinner?" I wouldn't have ended up there either.

I was the first woman to occupy the physical office whose previous inhabitants included George Stephanopoulos, Rahm Emmanuel, Karl Rove, David Axelrod, and David Plouffe. That might mean something to you, or it might not mean anything at all. It's not exactly the kind of job six-year-olds are naming for the "What do you want to be when you grow up?" question. It's not even the kind of job precocious 26-year-olds are gunning for. Most people who hear the title don't really know what I did. (Though they know enough to be impressed—especially if you say it kind of loudly, while raising your eyebrows and making a big gesture.) Jobs like this—the kind of job of which there are many, the kind that are definitely good but that no one teaches you to want—are found only with an open mind and a willingness to do your own thing.

One of my biggest advantages is that I was raised to be independent. (Not having Google around to answer any question that might have occurred to me helped.) My pop put himself through college stocking shelves in a liquor warehouse. My mom went to fashion school, worked until the day before she went into labor with me, and saved enough money from her job to buy our first house. A story I grew up hearing about my Omie is that after spending time helping Jews leave Germany before the war, she fled the country—her home— by herself, traveling through Switzerland and the UK with only my uncle Dieter, who was a baby at the time. One of the few possessions she had with her was a set of aquamarines; she hid them in his diaper. These are good role models.

Here's a childhood anecdote that is kind of corny but very useful in constructing a metaphor: I was probably two or three years old, and Omie, my mom, and I were at the 44 Plaza shopping center in Poughkeepsie around the holidays. We had just parked the Chevy Malibu and were crossing the parking lot to the Hallmark store when my grandma told me, "*Schatzi*, hold Omie's hand."

"No, Omie!" I said. "I hold my own hand!"

She promptly grabbed me by the hood, but I did hold my own hand.

It's kind of like life, right? We start by holding our own hands, kind of knowing someone has got us by the hood. I later tried to touch some crystal ornaments in the Hallmark store, and the hand I was holding myself with was smacked—an apt illustration of how independence can get you in trouble sometimes. (I never touched crystal ornaments at Hallmark ever again.)

* * *

Things were cruising until my sister Moosie was born. Moosie's real name is Lauren, but one Sunday morning when my pop was testing me on my middle-school French vocabulary, he pointed to a grapefruit on the table. Lauren was walking down the stairs as I said *pamplemousse*, and she replied, "I am not a plump little moose!" She is 36 years old now and still Moose.

But back to 1980. I don't really remember my mom being pregnant or the fact that she was having a baby. I do remember the night she went into labor: We packed up the car and Mom and Pop dropped me off at Mrs. Endsley's house. Kimmie Endsley was my best friend, and her older sister, Kristen, was really cool. I got to try Lucky Charms for the first time. (At 19 Vincent Road we had only Cheerios and Rice Krispies.) These were the true benefits to having a little sister!

When my mom called to say Moose had arrived, Mrs. Endsley asked me if I wanted to talk to her. I really didn't want to. Kimmie and I were having so much fun! But I did. I heard I had a sister.

I also heard that Omie and Opie were driving up from

New Jersey. JACKPOT AGAIN. Omie brought me a tea set as a present for becoming a big sister. We washed the drapes. It was the best.

Then Moose came home. Even when I was four, I knew she was cute—big cheeks, bigger thighs, and a huge head. She was really tan. All of this annoyed me. Her room was painted yellow, which annoyed me more, because my room was white, which seemed, at the time, objectively worse. (Looking back, her room was basically mustard yellow, so I don't know why I cared.) I did not want to hang out with her—I was *with* Omie, in the way that you are *with* people when you're young. I was very possessive, which was OK, because I was four years old, and although I had my independent streak, I didn't understand that the grown-ups had lives and preferences and friends they occasionally met up with for lunch or a walk (or some wine). I was the favorite, and I had to continue to be the favorite. Moose had only been around for a few days and really only pooped!

A little while after she was born, I think this attitude was showing. I remember brushing my teeth on my stepstool—it read, "To sit / To stand / This stool is really grand"—and I had a ponytail. My mom came in, gently grabbed my ponytail, and said, "This attitude ends today." After that, I tried to think about—at age four—the upside of being a big sister. Maybe there were perks? Maybe this was someone who would be required by blood to always think I was cooler and smarter?

Um, not the case. Moosie turned out to be taller, thinner, and a terrific dancer who always won awards. She was also a little aggressive. When she would get mad, she would roll down the hall in her walker and bite my bed. She liked to eat dirt from the houseplants and carry around a small bottle of bourbon (unopened). Her claim to fame was being called out at Freedom Plains Nursery School for getting on a tricycle and plowing through a castle some kid had built. You really never want her mad at you—she'll just stop talking to you.

(Now, Moosie and I talk almost every day. She can tell when I'm upset by how I punctuate my text messages and is always quick to suggest a mani-pedi or some Shake Shack to lift my spirits. When she got married, I toiled for two weeks to make my homemade granola and thyme-roasted marcona almonds as favors for all the guests.)

* * *

Being the oldest, as any oldest would attest, is a lot like being a pioneer. My first day of kindergarten was eye-opening, a wonder. Kindergarten was where I realized that, aside from the occasional "good girl Twinkie," we ate really healthily in my house. There was a much more exciting culinary world out there.

I liked school a lot, and I loved to read. I read way ahead of my grade level, but my mom never censored my books. I loved Judy Blume, and I think I was pretty young when I read *Are You There God? It's Me, Margaret*—the edition from the early '70s, where they still explained that maxi pads had belts. Maxi pads used to be held in place with a weird string-and-loop system, and that is what I learned about.

By the time I actually got my period, I was very confused. Where were the belts?

Around first grade, I wanted to join Girl Scouts, so I became a Brownie. This may have been the very first time I noticed a theme in my life that would go on to fail me again and again: Everyone was doing it, so I wanted to try, too.

Back in the early '80s, getting promoted to Girl Scout wasn't just about being old enough—you had to sell enough cookies. When the time came to sell those damn things, my mom made it clear she wasn't going to lift a finger, aside from buying the Thin Mints, Samoas, and Tagalongs we would have bought anyway. She wasn't going to pimp my cookies for me. Not like our dance instructor—let's call her Barb—who would put her daughter's order form at the door so parents could fill it out. Once the cookies arrived for distribution, Barb's dance studio looked like a Girl Scout Costco—Do-si-dos were flying everywhere. (Peanut allergy awareness was much lower than it is today.)

I, however, was on my own. For all the talents I may claim to have, sales is not one of them. Even today, I cannot stand fund-raising or asking people for things. I didn't make these cookies. What did I really care if I didn't sell them?

Mom and Pop got me a walkie-talkie and sent me up and down Vincent Road, the gospel of Thin Mints playing on repeat in my brain—*you can keep them in the freezer and save them for months!*—as if I were not a five-year-old kid but a stressed-out mother of two looking to streamline her cookie storage processes. I was not good. I was quite bad. We lived in a neighborhood with lots of Girl Scouts, making competition stiff and plentiful, but that wasn't really my problem. No, my approach was flawed: I mostly stood at a lot of front doors without ringing the bell.

I never made it to Girl Scout. When it was time to congratulate all the girls in my troop for selling exemplary numbers of cookies, I got a little award that was different from everyone else's.

This experience, while inducing a tear or two from five-year-old me, was beneficial: It taught me that failure was survivable, that it wouldn't ruin my life. (It helped, of course, that my mom did buy those few boxes, which I snacked from to console myself.) I failed on my own. I didn't think Barb's daughter was such a genius—her mom did all her work! I also learned at a young age that I was not, and never would be, a saleswoman. An easy thing to cross off the list of potential futures.

*　*　*

Over the years, my parents let me hold my own hand a lot. I think they always just hoped my sister and I would turn out to be good people—they didn't care about how successful or prominent or wealthy we would be. For example: dance classes, the extracurricular of choice (or parental pressure) for countless young girls, no matter your generational era. I took tap, ballet, and jazz for almost 12 years, and what I lacked in natural ability, I made up for in enthusiasm. I rationalized that I danced in the wings at our finales because of my height. I assumed that if I was sweating, I was succeeding.

Moosie, though, was a killer. A really great dancer. As I got older, I realized—partially because I could see an example of someone who was so suited to dance, unlike me—that I was investing a lot of time, hours and hours each week, in something I wasn't that good at and not enjoying all that much. It actually made me feel bad. I never had a solo.

I was 16 when I finally told my mom I wanted to quit. Although quitting is a thing many people now are taught to never, ever do, she didn't flip out. She didn't lose her mind or berate me about having extracurriculars on my college applications or say I had been dancing for so long that I should keep going. She said it was OK. If you do it responsibly, quitting something that isn't benefiting you—whether it's dance classes that "everyone is taking" or a soul-sucking job that has nothing to do with anything you're interested in—can change your life.

After I finished dance, I didn't sit around eating Now and Laters and cruising the highways and byways of Rhinebeck. I was first flute in the band in school. I took French. I babysat for a family down the street every Saturday night, and I also worked at their anemone barn. I would wrap the flowers in wet paper towels and newspapers to prepare them for long trips back to the city with tourists every Sunday. This wasn't some bougie "barn"—it was an actual barn, with power tools and a tiny space heater. My best friend, Cara, visited me every weekend and brought me soup or donuts or a bagel. I loved it there.

I also had a job as a checker at Kilmer's IGA Market, a grocery store in the center of town. Anyone who has worked at Kmart or Walmart or their own local grocery store may not believe me when I say this, but I really liked it. Sure, some days you definitely want to hang with your friends instead, but I was good at bagging groceries, and it meant I could afford tickets to see Phish or God Street Wine or the Dead. I could buy crystals—they were cool then, too—and smock dresses from Winter Sun.

I also learned a lot about people. What they bought. Who used coupons and who didn't. Who helped you pack and who just stood there and waited. Who watched you scan every item and questioned the price.

Our store was one of only a few that accepted food stamps in the area, which gave me more perspective than almost anything else I experienced growing up. It's a moment when you see a woman with a kid, or an older person, trying to figure out what the food stamps cover. The humiliation they can endure while holding up the line, or having to put things back. It forever formed my opinion on how we should help those in need: humanely and respectfully. Maybe that sounds obvious to you, but unfortunately there are a lot of people who would disagree.

Years later, we were having a discussion about food stamps in the White House. My job was never policy focused; I scheduled and coordinated and planned, dealing with times and dates as well as with personalities. But I often sat in on policy meetings so that I could understand our priorities and be able to use my judgment as my team decided, out of a hundred different choices per day, how best to use POTUS's time. This discussion was a follow-up to a conversation Obama had had with someone else; often he'd gather senior staff to talk over issues as a group after meeting with a particular person.

Because of the economic recession, there were a lot of people on food stamps at the beginning of Obama's presidency. That number dropped over his term, but we didn't only have meetings about what was happening right at that moment, because if you're just dealing with things as they're happening, you aren't prepared for something to come out of the blue. This meeting was in the Roosevelt Room, but I wasn't sitting at the table—I was sitting along the wall. Seating is surprisingly limited in the West Wing—the chairs are huge and not that many fit around the conference tables, many of which are historical or have some other kind of significance, so invitations to meetings are kind of exclusive. Everyone in the room needs to have a good reason for being there.

From the beginning of my career in politics, I had a personally imposed policy about swimming in my lane and not overcommenting on things I wasn't an expert on. But in this case, I could not take the pontifications of this Ivy-educated gang; they were talking about the limits on what food stamps cover and don't, and I could just tell none of them knew one person who had ever needed food stamps. I raised my hand (something I think only I did when I wanted to talk) and told them what it was like to see people humiliated in line trying to buy generic cereal, canned soup, milk. To watch them realize what they couldn't get. To watch them realize how ridiculous it was that sports drinks were covered but something like Sunny Delight—which is actually much cheaper than orange juice but still has a decent amount of vitamins—was not, but that there was nothing they could do. I could feel my face get red and hot. I usually think you start losing your argument when you physically reveal how worked up you are, especially in a place like the White House, where, theoretically, what you say should be based on facts and figures and evidence; if your face is red, aren't you showing too much emotion? I don't know, but I got my point across. It wasn't a conversation intended to resolve or change anything at that moment, but POTUS made it clear he was on my side.

■　■　■

The best part about those jobs in high school—all of which I gained some satisfaction from and remember fondly, even if at the time I was thinking I would rather be watching *90210*—was that they taught me a very important way to rationalize when my career seemed doomed or my life felt like it was veering totally off course: *If I am never good at anything else, I know I am good at this.* You might think that sounds depressing, but it's given me a lot of comfort over the years. There is no greater feeling of independence than being able to provide for yourself, knowing that if you really hate a job—and you will probably hate jobs at various points throughout your life—you can leave and be OK.

When it came time for me to apply to college, I had one of those moments where I needed to remember that, at the end of the day, at least I was really good at bagging groceries. That if I didn't get into Harvard (or even choose to apply), I would end up where I was supposed to end up.

The time period was 1992–94; there was no email, no

Internet. We drove to Barnes & Noble and bought the *US News* college guidebook. Cara and I spent hours and hours tagging pages and talking about where we wanted to go. I underlined addresses and, in the summer before my senior year, wrote away to request applications.

As a family, we picked a few schools to visit—Georgetown, Berkeley, Stanford, UC Santa Cruz. I didn't end up applying to all of them, but the places I did apply to—University of Vermont, University of Wisconsin, Cornell, Brown, Georgetown, SUNY Albany, and Fairfield—I did myself. I wrote the essays, which no one proofread, and studied for the SATs and did pretty well. (Especially in verbal.) My mom did help me fill out the checks for the application fees—and disclaimer: They were my mom's checks.

If you haven't seen *St. Elmo's Fire*, you won't really be able to fully understand my mind-set at the time, but I really wanted to go to Georgetown. The movie takes place in the year after a group of friends graduates from there and tries to find their way in the world. For some reason, even though I hadn't really thought much about getting into politics at the time, I wanted to be Alec; he was a very self-important 22-year-old working on a congressional campaign and cheating on his live-in girlfriend, Ally Sheedy, who was too good for him. The characters were very weird role models: They drank a lot, a couple of them did a lot of coke, and they spent too much money. But they were attractive and funny and ultimately made it out alive. I credited all this to the fact that they had gone to Georgetown. I thought that if I got in I would be able to access some of that Brat Pack energy.

I was top 10 in my class (and by top 10, I mean number 11 of 76) and not short on confidence. Who wouldn't want me?

I got all my rejections on the same day in April. After returning from our second pilgrimage to Georgetown, where I had bought a car sticker because I was so convinced I was going to get in, we got home to realize the cashier had forgotten to put the sticker in our bag. Later, when my dad got the mail and I opened my very thin letter from Georgetown—and all the others—we realized it was a sign. (Signs like this work only in retrospect.)

I ended up choosing between the University of Vermont and the University of Wisconsin–Madison. Coming from such a small town, I was worried I would be too fish-out-of-water-y in Madison, so I happily and proudly signed up to be a Catamount in the freshman class of 1994. When I sent in the forms to register for housing, a meal plan, all that stuff that makes you feel like your new life is about to start, I had never set foot on campus.

Sometimes I do leap and then look, for better or for worse. Sometimes it works out great. Other times…maybe things could have gone a little better.

If I had a sense of myself in high school, I lost it in college. This was the first time I realized that money mattered and how you spent it mattered more, and since my family put value on getting the most out of your car—I thought Ford Taurus station wagons were aces because they lasted forever—I had no idea who I was. I grew up in a town where you didn't know who had money and who didn't. The wealthiest families were probably the equine veterinarians, and they drove beat-up Suburbans and Wagoneers. I don't really remember anyone wearing makeup, save a little cover-up for sweet teen acne. I wore clothes from the Gap or Marshalls, and my hairstyle rode the wave from Magic Mushroom bowl cut to Eddie Vedder shag. (Think about it: When his hair was shorter, the layers were very similar to the Rachel.)

It wasn't all bad. I was good friends with my roommate, Amy, and our floor had a lot of Joni Mitchell and Indigo Girls listening sessions, and a lot of talks about "what bugged you out." The mid-'90s "bug out" could describe any number of situations: when you encountered someone weird, when you smoked bad pot, when you experienced your first bout of insomnia because the guy in Intro Psych didn't sit next to you and you just couldn't figure out why. In retrospect, this was very fun.

My classes helped me branch out, too. I majored in French and also became very good at Japanese, which I signed up for on a whim. One semester I took a course in rural sociology, which focused on poverty in the Northeast Kingdom of Vermont, and I later used what I'd learned to make small talk with Oprah while we waited for an Obama event in Iowa to start.

Still, around the beginning of sophomore year, I began to realize my French major was maybe not taking me in the direction I wanted to go. Vermont is very political—people say what they think. They disagree without being disagreeable and have discussions without fighting. State and local officials were always on campus; Governor Howard Dean came to register us to vote; I got to jump on a reviled Republican's car. I found myself gravitating toward the political stuff, whether it was on or off campus. That winter, I decided to apply for a summer internship with Bernie Sanders.

When spring break rolled around, I found out that the budget for the French department was being cut and it might not be offered as a major any longer. I thought this was a sign, so I reapplied to the University of Wisconsin–Madison to transfer in my junior year, and I was accepted. A few weeks later, I also got the Bernie Sanders internship, working from May through August in his Burlington congressional office.

The internship didn't pay, but I was able to stay with a couple of friends in Burlington, in an apartment on South Street behind a liquor store. I slept on a futon and more than once woke up to see a spider I had crushed in my sleep.

But it didn't matter: Nothing had ever been more exciting. It was an election year, so Bernie was in the office a lot, and he met with constituents more than any politician I've known since. I was kept very busy, which I loved. I answered phones and took down notes from voters. I faxed press clips. I filed. At night, I would call people in all parts of Vermont, trying to raise money. I wasn't super successful, but I did a great job at reminding people to register to vote and telling them about events Bernie would be doing around the state.

From time to time, I also got to drive Bernie around. He looked the same way he looks now—super disheveled, his tie a little loose, always brusque but fair. He would usually read the newspaper, even though we always had the windows down—never air-conditioning. Sometimes he asked about my family, and where I was from, and explained to me what was going on in the world. I once tried to impress him by telling him about the time my friends and I had climbed on Newt Gingrich's car. Bernie was unmoved; his attitude was basically, "Well, what else would you have been doing?"

Before I met Bernie, I had always thought politics was about theater and showmanship and that nothing really happened or got fixed. But instead of focusing on the large-scale changes many people expect from politicians, he showed me how to see the people whose problems he could immediately impact and solve. The people who worked for him also seemed genuinely dedicated to helping his constituents, which is not necessarily true of other senators; many politicians have staffs made up of climbers, who move from one senator to another to get up the ladder, with the ultimate goal of becoming a legislative director or chief of staff. (Of course, some politicians' staff members want to go on and run for office themselves, but a lot of times ambition in Washington is just about being powerful, and you can be powerful without a seat in Congress.) Bernie was so committed to his issues, and to Vermont, that politics didn't feel gross. Before I left for Madison, I changed my major to political science.

One day at the end of my internship, two important things happened. The first was that I saw a call come in for Bernie from a 608 area code, which was Madison. Bernie was running late, so I told the man on the line, Ed Garvey, that he might have to wait a few minutes.

In the meantime, I asked questions. I always tried to learn about the people coming into the office, especially people meeting with or talking to Bernie; I wanted to know what made them important enough to warrant his time and attention. I researched everything I could.

So when I got Ed on the phone and he had to wait, I saw my chance. I knew that Ed was a very important labor attorney; he had unionized the NFL Players Association and was a progressive leader in Madison. I told him that I was going to be transferring to Madison in a month. He replied that I should come see him when I arrived on campus. I worked for him for the two years I lived there.

* * *

The other important thing that happened that day was that Bernie's team invited me to be an intern in their DC office the following summer. I don't know if anyone in that office will ever understand what that meant to me. I felt like Wonder Woman. I was ready to strike out. I packed up and went back to Rhinebeck for a week or two, and then we drove out to Madison.

I saved all my money that year—from working for Ed Garvey, from babysitting for a family outside of Madison a couple of times a week, and all of what I got for my 21st birthday—for my summer in DC. I lived in Tenleytown with a friend from Rhinebeck, Shannon, who was going to law school at American. I drove to the metro, parked, and took the train to Capitol South. I had exactly five outfits to rotate each week. I made tomato and mayonnaise sandwiches and packed some pretzels for snacks.

I walked into Bernie's office feeling ready to jam, but this was a way different vibe. These interns were kind of competitive, and I'd rather bang in a drum circle all day than ever have to compete. I had a minor crisis of confidence. Then I remembered that I knew a hundred times more about Vermont than these guys.

I was busy every day walking briskly and professionally over the halls of Congress. Getting signatures on bills or amendments. Running anything and everything to other offices and helping to draft letters to constituents. If *Legally Blonde* had come out by then, I would have fancied myself a version of Elle Woods meets Norma Rae, the union organizer. When my internship ended—and I was basically out of money—I was convinced I would be back the following summer after graduation to start my career as a humble and committed government employee. I didn't get to interact with Bernie that much, but it didn't really matter: Working for him had given me back a clear picture of who I was and what I wanted to do.

CHAPTER 4

Self-awareness, or Are You There, FEMA? It's Me, Alyssa

By the end of my senior year at Madison, I knew I needed to start planning for graduation and the new life I had fully envisioned for myself in DC, so I went to the career office to figure out how to apply for jobs. I wrote cover letters and attached my 22-year-old's résumé, which still included hostessing, babysitting, and being a checker at Kilmer's. I was confident; I had worked hard, I was proud of what I'd done for Bernie, and I was certain I wanted to be in government. I applied to be the person who answered the phones for every member of Congress from New York State, Wisconsin, and Vermont. I applied to work for the Democratic National Committee and Democratic Senatorial Campaign Committee. I had no delusions of grandeur. I would have just been happy to be there.

No one called me. No one wrote me back. I called my friends in Bernie's office, and they broke the news that they weren't filling any junior positions.

The lease in Madison was up in mid-August. What the hell was I going to do?

Young people are not known for their acute sense of self-awareness, and I was no exception. Unfortunately, that's by design; you haven't had a lot of time to get to know yourself yet. The only way to get through periods of confusion like the one I'm about to describe is to ask yourself a bunch of questions and slowly find the answers to them. Who am I? What do I want in life? What am I good at? What am I bad at? Does my hair actually look good with so many layers? Do I care?

To encourage me, in a backhanded kind of way, my pop told me this story about when he graduated from NYU. He had offers for jobs in Hartford, but he really wanted a full-time job at IBM. He was waiting to hear from IBM, but he knew he might have to go to Hartford.

Capitol Hill was my IBM. I thought, *Is Pop telling me to go to Hartford?*

He was. (Though he himself did not end up having to go to Hartford.)

Before my lease was up, I flew from Madison to Rhinebeck and took the train down to Manhattan to see some headhunters.

Headhunters are rough. It's their job to get you to take a job, so telling you how amazing you are isn't on the top of their list; they want you to feel grateful for whatever they land you. And in my case, it was my job as a paralegal at Thacher Proffitt & Wood. My salary was $26,000 and I was eligible for overtime. I had no idea what that meant.

I went back to Madison and accepted that I wasn't going to work in Congress—maybe ever—but I was going to be an awesome paralegal. Even though I had no idea what that meant, either. My mom took me shopping, and I got a brown suede suit from Banana Republic that I wore on my first day, even though it was about 85 degrees outside.

I did my training with Volpes and Kara O'Leary (Kolea), who was also very cool. A woman named Emma taught us all about Redwelds (accordion folders with ties on them), why you always wanted to have enough lobster traps (metal accordion folders that hold closing documents and keep them orderly), and how to do a Uniform Commercial Code (UCC) filing. The UCC governs commercial transactions in the United States; in 1998, UCCs still had to be done on the typewriter for carbon copies (like physical carbon copies) for Arizona, New Jersey, and Massachusetts, and I did a lot of them. This advice was more relevant a few years ago, but still: Never brag about your ability to type. It will never get you anywhere you really want to be.

I was not rushing back and forth through the halls of Congress, but I was in the World Trade Center, helping lawyers close deals for millions of dollars. That was something, right?

After about a year, paralegals cycle out. Volpes got into law school. Kolea was moving to Buffalo ("the Buff") to live with her boyfriend (now husband). Because I had spent a lot of time at bars in the Financial District surrounded by finance people, I decided to leave for a job at Merrill Lynch.

"Wait," you say. "What?" No fucking idea. My friends were leaving, and I had to go, too. Months earlier, I had gone through an arduous interview process to become an assistant in International Paper Trading at Lehman Brothers, only to make it to the bitter end and decide that I absolutely did not want to do that. But working in finance seemed like something a "successful" person would do, and everyone in my crew was doing something new, so I gave it another shot. (In case you were curious, Investopedia defines "paper trading" as the practice of "using simulated trading to practice buying and selling securities without using any actual money." It lets investors practice trading, basically. I know more about paper trading from looking it up to try to explain it here than I did when I was interviewing for the job.)

The headhunter got me an interview at Merrill Lynch, which was in the World Financial Center, right across from the World Trade Center. I don't remember much about the process, except that I was offered $35,000 to be an assistant to the managing director in rubber, which I think means that his group analyzed rubber sales and the cost of buying rubber globally. I was really wowed by the salary, which is insane, since I made a base of $26,000 at TPW and got overtime, which meant I grossed about $42,000 in 12 months. Why the hell did I care about $35,000? I got to $42K working crazy hours; this job was not eligible for overtime, which meant that no matter how many hours I worked, I would only get $35K.

In the interview, I did not ask questions. They kept talking about me being "support," and at one point they asked me how many words I could type per minute, but I didn't think about it. I was determined to work in finance, and I would do whatever that meant when the time came.

On my first day, a woman from Human Resources took me to my desk, and I saw that it was a desk among many desks that sat outside offices, like in *Mad Men*. You never want to be able to compare your work environment to *Mad Men*. As in *Mad Men*, all the desks were occupied by women. Some very simple but useful advice: Always ask to see where you'll be sitting.

My heart started to race. I had taken the job thinking I would be the most junior person on the rubber team. What I had not realized, but what my security badge made crystal clear, was that I had taken a job as the rubber team's secretary.

I told myself I had made my bed and now it was time to lie in it. I sat down. I programmed my voice mail. I got the password to my computer. I tried to care about what people were saying to me. But I didn't.

I knew I would regret it if I stayed, but I also had about $65 in my checking account and no savings to speak of. I don't know why, honestly. My friends and I didn't go out to eat much or buy fancy things; taking a taxi to the Upper East Side was seen as a luxury and treated that way. But in New York there is like a $10 toll just for stepping out of your apartment. (Today it's more like $25.)

I called my mom and dad to tell them I had been duped— well, it was probably my fault, but that isn't what I told them—and had to quit. I said I might need some money, and they said to ask if I did, but I didn't want to have to.

I quit by leaving a voice mail on my boss's office line at the end of my first week (don't do this) and never went back there again.

It was the infernal New York summer, and our apartment didn't have air-conditioning. Because I was sitting around in it all day, I quickly broke down and used $30 of the $65 in my checking account to buy an oscillating fan. I had the fan less than 24 hours before my roommate decided to do some cooking in our 75-square-foot living room/kitchen and moved it onto the hot stove. It melted and became a crooked fan that couldn't oscillate.

Every morning, I would go out to get a paper or magazine—*Village Voice, Daily News, Post, New York Times*—to check for job listings, which I would go through at the coffee place Cara and I called Suspect Coffee—an equivalent nickname today might be Sketch Coffee. It was kind of vicious of us, since Adam, the guy who worked there, gave me the day-old corn muffins for free after he noticed that I was coming in at around 9:30 instead of my usual 7:00 and I told him it was because I was now unemployed.

I took the free corn muffins and interviewed at loads of places. Tokyo Mitsubishi Bank (I ended up doing a Japanese minor). Some French mineral company. Another place that had something to do with rubber. I ended up as the assistant to the CEO at an Internet start-up called SenseNet on Hudson Street. I had no interest in the Internet, or venture capital, or really anything I was doing, but the people were nice and I could wear whatever I wanted to work and it was within walking distance of our apartment. Sometimes, for a little while, that's enough. Though I didn't make much money, I was diligent about putting $10 or $20 aside whenever I could. I never wanted my corn muffins to be in jeopardy again.

A BRIEF INTERLUDE ON HOW TO BE
RESPONSIBLE WITH MONEY

It's not very sexy to think about personal finance,
which is why so many people have no control over theirs.
Unfortunately, it never really gets fun! But there are things
you need in your back pocket in order to live life how you
want. I didn't have any of them when I left the job as
rubber secretary at Merrill Lynch.

First, your credit score matters, and monitoring it is your
job. (Checking your credit score doesn't lower your score,
which is a common misconception I believed for a long
time.) I would flag this as a major item for anyone looking to
work on a campaign or at a start-up, where things can be a
little "loose."

For example: When I was on the Kerry campaign in 2003,
I managed our relationship with our air charter company.
A senior person on the campaign told me I would get my
own credit card. Awesome, right? No. From what I can
re-create of the disaster, my social security number was
used to get the card. This card had a balance of roughly
$150,000 in charter fees at any time. At the end of 2003,
we wanted to show a lot of cash on hand in our campaign
bank accounts—a sign of viability when the numbers are
publicly released at the end of each quarter—so we did not
pay the air charter bill for about two months. This meant

that for more than 60 days, I had an outstanding balance of about $500,000.

It completely destroyed my personal credit, and I only found out months later, when I wrecked the Toyota Corolla my pop gave me and was rejected for a $5,000 auto loan when I tried to buy another car; I got to work so early and left so late that a car was a necessity, not a luxury. It had not occurred to me that they were using my social security number to get the card—I should have guarded it with my life.

Second, savings. I'm sure you've all read about having a "Fuck You account." If not: A Fuck You account is the money you keep around in case you need to say "Fuck you!" to someone or something, fast—a boyfriend or girlfriend, a terrible job, a shitty landlord. The more money you have in savings, the more mental space you can give yourself in making decisions, and the more secure you'll feel. I babysat after work a few nights a week and on Saturdays until my schedule absolutely did not allow it—through my entire time in Boston working for John Kerry and for many of my first years in DC. After the Summer of Unemployment, I vowed to always have money in the bank, no matter what— even though I never had a job that paid well until a few years ago.

I was especially diligent about putting money away on the Kerry campaign after the car debacle. (I used the $1,500 I had in savings to buy a 1988 Saab. This was early 2004.) Working on a campaign is very risky, in terms of job security as well as salary—your employment is guaranteed only as long as your candidate is alive and has a chance at winning. (This is even truer today: With social media and a 24/7 news cycle, it doesn't take much to start losing.) By the time the campaign ended in defeat, I had about $3,000 in my savings account, which was enough to pay my rent and expenses (on Campbell's soup, PB&J, and, as a treat, McDonald's) for about three months. When Tey and I drove out to Anacostia to sign up for unemployment, there was a line in the office just for Kerry campaign people. I didn't sign up, and I don't think she did either. We were convinced we would get our shit settled before we ran out of money.

Luckily, we both did—Tey started working for Senator Maria Cantwell, and I started working for Senator Obama a month or so later. But in the meantime, I never bought coffee out, got a manicure, or went to the grocery store without coupons. Like I said, not sexy.

* * *

I really liked New York City, even if it is a hard place to truly succeed. I took early Saturday morning walks up to Central Park. We explored weird little bars (only after pregaming with some cheap booze and Crystal Light to ensure we had to purchase only one drink when we were out) and ate gravy fries at Milady's (sadly, no longer around) when we were feeling fancy or got a paycheck. Otherwise, we would have a lot of turkey sandwiches from M & O Market on Thompson Street, or tuna on Wasa crackers with mustard. My favorite memory is when Cara and I played hooky from work and ate at the Cub Room (also no longer around). We had cocktails during the day, which was very exciting to me at the time. (I feel like day drinking really only came into its own a few years ago).

The thing is, though: The work scene at SenseNet wasn't me, and it kind of bummed me out; I was beginning to think nothing was really me. I did what I was supposed to (filing, faxing, answering phones, learning about "the Internet," making appointments and lunch reservations) with a good attitude, but it was not even remotely stimulating. I left after a few months—a few months after that, SenseNet was bought by another company and everyone got really rich—and got a job at Sotheby's.

"Wait," you're saying again. "What?" Why not! I did client relations in the international realty division. The money was fine, the wardrobe was at least somewhat relaxed, and it took me to a different part of town—the Upper East Side.

By this point, bouncing back and acclimating had become my thing. I made fast friends at Sotheby's. My boss was Tom; he was really intense and loved his job a lot. I couldn't understand how anyone could feel so passionately about real estate, but he did, and instead of mocking his love of luxury property, I went with it. I learned a lot about the difference between mansions, estates, cottages, and "important homes." It's best to have your home oriented toward the sun (though one must be careful of too much southern exposure). "Historic" is often code for "money pit." I listened closely as Tom talked his clients through their options. Now, 18 years later, I've had the opportunity to impress a lot of doubtful men with weird factoids and assessments.

I was there for a few months, and I got pretty good at real estate. I liked making brochures and talking to clients; I had my favorite properties. It was really pretty fun.

But a few months earlier, I had visited Volpes in Boston, where I saw John Kerry give a speech on TV. *What if?* There was nothing really remarkable about the speech, but I had not seen a political speech in so long that I had almost forgotten how exciting it was to hear someone talk about possibility and change—to hear something aspirational. I felt like myself for the first time in a long time.

I sent a letter to his intern coordinator in the winter of 2000. I say "letter," but it was really more of a plea. I said that I knew I was meant to work in government, and that I would do anything to make it happen. I said I was willing to intern even though I'd been out of college for a couple of years, and I wasn't just bullshitting. My internship for Bernie was more satisfying than most of the jobs I'd had, and I had done it while earning enough for rent and expenses with a smattering of supplemental jobs—I could do that again. I was convinced that if I could just get my foot in the door, I would end up with a job.

About two or three weeks later, I came home from work to a message on our answering machine: Someone at Senator Kerry's office wanted to discuss my interest in working there. (Note the difference between "interest" and any mention of an actual job.) At long last, after a series of roles that seemingly made no sense and that I took for no good reason, I got the call I had dreamed of. Sort of.

I went up to Boston twice for interviews. The first time was sort of "informational"—but you should treat anything called "informational" as the real deal, because you never know. I wore the brown suit. I brought fresh copies of my résumé on good paper. I read up on everything and anything John Kerry. I even memorized a few quotes that his press secretary, Kyle Sullivan, had given to the *Boston Globe*. (This was before the real Internet, so I actually had to buy copies of the paper and scan the clips.) These were adults taking time out of their day to meet with me, and I was going to attack the meeting.

A few weeks later, I made a second trip, and I met with the state director, the press secretary, and the scheduler. I dropped all the information I could mostly casually fit into the conversation, but I also conveyed that I would do whatever it took to make the most of the opportunity. I talked about "no job being too small for me," and I remember saying to them, "If I can't answer the phones right or get the clips done on time, why would you give me anything else to do?"

Self-awareness—it always impresses people. I did end up answering the phones a lot. Before I left that second interview, Senator Kerry walked into the room. He blew past me and into his office, but then I heard him ask who I was. His team told him I was interviewing. He asked for my résumé, and I heard him say, "She worked at Sotheby's—she must be good." Forward motion is always better than no motion— even if you don't think it's taking you in the direction you wanted to go.

I got a call a few days later from Jeff, the state director, and he offered me the position of assistant to the press department and the scheduler. I would take shifts answering the phones and dealing with mail for $20,500 a year. I did not hesitate in thanking them for this blessed opportunity and immediately started thinking about ways I could spice up Top Ramen. I was totally giddy. My last week at Sotheby's coincided with the series finale of *90210*.

* * *

I have learned a lot about myself over the years, mostly because I was open to hearing feedback. I wear my emotions on my sleeve. I usually dislike someone before I like them. I'm sensitive—especially when I'm tired or feel I'm being misunderstood. This may sound like the "About Me" section on a bad online dating profile, but knowing this stuff has allowed me to keep my contacts, my reputation, and my sanity throughout a long and often stressful career. Being self-aware means knowing when you're about to act bad—and then not acting bad.

In the summer of 2012, the White House was in the middle of a reelection, so I had to coordinate plans related to that on top of my ordinary responsibilities. Here's a typical day:

650AM: Drive through West Exec gates to ensure my parking spot
655AM: Grab a latte at Navy Mess
700AM: Read national security book or press clips, or watch the news
730AM: Senior advisers meeting in the chief of staff's office
830AM: Senior staff meeting in the Roosevelt Room

905AM: Ask Clay why my English muffin is cold / Talk to Kathy and Pfeiffer about latest episode of *Girls* (seriously)

1000AM: Meeting with WH Office of Management and Administration (M+A)

1050AM: Talk to Clay and Pfeiffer about lunch orders and discuss soups of the day

1100AM: POTUS meeting with senior advisers

AM/PM: Weekly planning brainstorming meeting (small)

AM/PM: Weekly planning in the chief of staff's office

AM/PM: Weekly nominations and confirmations meeting

AM/PM: Weekly Cabinet affairs update meeting

AM/PM: Weekly WHMO update

AM/PM: NSC weekly planning meeting

600PM: Wrap-up in chief of staff's office (it was anyone's guess what time this would actually start)

730/800PM: Walk through door / feed cat / uncork wine

In 2012, we traveled so much that, often, many of the weekly meetings would have to be packed into one day, or done from AF1 or by phone in the motorcade. Then you layer in coordinating (lawfully) with the campaign, Obama for America (OFA), so you don't fuck up their mission (get Obama reelected) and they don't fuck up yours (keep the government running so that Obama will get reelected so you can keep the government running). I managed the interactions between our Cabinet secretaries and the campaign, making sure that whatever they did—appearing at events for candidates, speaking at state party events, or doing fund-raisers—complied with the laws that cover government officials and political activity. It was not easy. One wrong word, and you could become a headline. I also worked with the Romney campaign to make sure that their most senior staff began getting national security clearances, to have that process under way in the event Romney won.

National security clearances are a funny and worrisome thing. Clearance begins with a form called the SF86, and, notoriously, there's a section that asks you about drug use.

I smoked a lot of pot growing up, in high school and college and afterward. I hadn't smoked *that much* on the campaign in 2008, but even then, I had done it. I didn't really think about it; obviously, when you're at the White House, you don't smoke it, but come on. Most of us on the Obama campaign had worked in the Senate before, so we thought we'd experienced what it's like to work in the national government, but we'd had no idea. The White House is a totally foreign place.

When I got the SF86, I freaked out. It asks what drugs you've done, and there's a place to write how many times you'd done them. I'm very honest, so next to marijuana, I wrote, "Unknown."

At times, I was able to pretend like the SF86 wasn't a big deal, just a normal bit of tedious bureaucracy, but I was terrified. It had never, ever occurred to me that marijuana was something that could keep you from a job. Was I going to have to tell my parents that I couldn't work in the White

House because I'd smoked pot? What lamer and more embarrassing experience could a person have?

Shortly after you fill out the form, an FBI agent interviews you. She brought in my form, and soon—I can't remember when in the interview; I only remember freaking out about the weed and babbling on about a time I accidentally went to a strip club in Miami with my friend Samantha—she asked how many times I had smoked pot.

I said I didn't know.

She said, "More than twenty?"

"Yes," I replied. "More than twenty."

"More than a hundred?" she asked. I was sweating.

"Yes," I said, dying. "More than a hundred."

"More than five hundred?"

"Just write 'unknown'!"

Do I think pot should be legal? Hell yes I do. Not to validate my use of it, but because I believe that it has health benefits, many more than some other substances that are legal. Was I aware of some of the risks of smoking pot when I did it? Yes. Had I known at age 18 that smoking some pot would be so impactful later in life, would I not have done it? Who knows. FBI agents had to contact all my friends to ask them if I had smoked weed; when I called these friends to prepare them, they were quick to assure me they would say they'd never seen me do it, and I had to tell them, "No! Please tell them that you've seen me do it!" (The government needs to see that employees can't be blackmailed, and that they aren't truly delinquent, or liars.) For the first year of my time in the White House, I was randomly drug tested almost every month.

Part of my job at the White House was vetting people's histories—relationships, interactions with foreign nationals, drug use, employment and housing history—to understand their fitness to work for the president. I saw some shit. Tax problems with nannies who applicants declare as employees but then obviously pay under the table. Weird personal web pages about practicing witchcraft. Those were the people who got left behind in the vetting meetings. But almost nothing I saw back then compares to what I see on Twitter or Instagram now. If I had to answer for photos I took in college (I speak mostly about the phase when I was dedicated to looking like Janeane Garofalo in *Reality Bites*), it honestly wouldn't be that bad. Things you say on Twitter are probably less shocking now than they were at the beginning of the administration, when social media was new, but if you want to work in public service, you still really have to be careful. You don't realize when you're just living your life that it can come back to haunt you. I recently saw a Twitter post from someone I know about doing cocaine in a foreign country. It's very hard to un-see those things.

※　※　※

The summer of 2012 was one of the most challenging periods of my professional life. While I was coordinating with the campaign and the Romney team, we went on a bus tour through Iowa. This was fun—we ate roasted turkey legs at the State Fair while Axelrod talked to Barbra Streisand on the phone. Then Benghazi happened: Islamic militants attacked the American diplomatic compound in Benghazi,

Libya, on September 11, 2012, killing the American ambassador to the country, a foreign service information management officer, and two CIA contractors. From there, we headed into the three presidential debates, and the first one, in Denver, didn't go so hot for us. POTUS came back with vigor at the second debate at Hofstra University, but a little more than a week before the election, Hurricane Sandy came barreling up the East Coast.

That close to an election, you have your core team in the White House making sure the government is still functioning as it should, but a lot of people are on the road—traveling with POTUS, doing Get Out the Vote, speaking at events, etc. When we were doing our transition meetings with the Bush administration back in 2009, they told us that Hurricane Katrina happened on a weekend many White House staff members were away; no one was making excuses, but they were paying forward a lesson: Make sure you always have a core decision-making team in the West Wing at all times.

As part of my job as deputy chief, I worked with FEMA, the Department of Homeland Security, and the National Security team on short-term and long-term responses to and recovery from natural disasters and coordinated those efforts across the administration. We also worked with state and local governments, local churches, nonprofits, and utilities companies. With climate change, it wasn't just Atlantic hurricane season (which runs from June 1 until November 30) that required more vigilance; there were year-round challenges. Droughts. Wildfires. Floods. You name it.

I had experience working on emergency management—I was with Obama when he was a senator during Hurricane Katrina, and I watched how he handled it. He really tried to listen to local citizens and officials to give them what they needed—not just what he thought they needed. When the storm hit, he was in Russia for the Senate Committee on Foreign Relations; he wanted to head straight to New Orleans from there, but we convinced him not to. We decided instead to work with a conservative senator from Mississippi, since most efforts were going to Louisiana and New Orleans specifically. I vividly remember being on a conference call and, in the middle of a discussion about how to send supplies to the area through the Mississippi senator's church in Pascagoula, hearing Obama say, "I want to make sure we're sending enough feminine products to the Gulf Coast. I've heard they really need that. Diapers and feminine products—that's what people need."

About a week before Sandy made landfall in the United States, we started talking with the National Weather Service, and we were getting reports that this was NOT A DRILL. A major storm was looking to impact the most densely populated part of the country less than two weeks before an election. Hurricane Sandy crossed over Puerto Rico on October 25, and by October 28, Governor Andrew Cuomo had ordered the MTA, which includes the New York subways, to close through at least October 30.

We needed to keep a lot of things in mind. We couldn't campaign anywhere that we might divert resources (police, first responders, ambulances) from storm prep or distract from evacuations. It was better for the president not to be on the East Coast at all, especially since the storm was going to blow through DC. If the storm were super bad in DC, he would have been stuck, so it was better to keep moving.

As much as I love campaigns and traveling with the president, it was on me to stay and literally weather the storm. In every crisis, you need a captain—a person who is constantly gathering all the available information, who knows the whole story and all its component parts, in order to make decisions holistically and keep everyone involved aware of what's going on.

As Sandy was bearing down on New York and New Jersey, it was still raining in DC, but the worst part of the storm had passed. Still, everything in DC was shut down—it was like a ghost town—and we could only get to work by having members of the military pick us up in Suburbans.

There was no point in having everyone in the office risk their lives so they could be in the White House—we have cell phones and wifi—so I told most people to stay home. But there was a handful of us left, and we all worked together from the comms office in the West Wing; there's no instant messaging in the White House, and it was easier to communicate this way. We tracked the storm's developments using the NY1, *New York Post*, *New York Daily News*, and CNN Twitter feeds (my first real interaction with Twitter) and shouted what we knew at one another. If I saw an official in Jersey City tweeting that he wasn't getting Red Cross trucks, someone else got on the phone with the Red Cross. And lo and behold, soon, the Red Cross trucks arrived on the scene.

During a natural disaster, the White House has several jobs. First and foremost, we try to make sure people understand the severity of what is about to happen without overreacting. In a post-Katrina world, the easiest thing to do on the eve of a major storm would be to evacuate, right? Not necessarily. If you order evacuations too often—and then the storm ends up being just a lot of rain—people will stop listening to the government. Evacuating is a big deal for a family, emotionally and logistically and financially. You never want people to become desensitized to or dismissive of what the government is recommending, but it is imperative to convey the gravity of the situation and make sure everyone understands the appropriate precautions to take. Once the storm passes, we act almost as a whip operation—ensuring that all administrative agencies are working as quickly and efficiently as possible to get help where it's needed.

Since I was running point for the White House, the campaign's message to me was not subtle: "DO NOT FUCK THIS UP." (There were far more important reasons than the election to not fuck it up, but you get a picture of what I was dealing with. When it comes to natural disasters, there's zero tolerance for presidential mistakes, so I really didn't need some passive-aggressive email to remind me of our responsibility.)

We were updating the president by phone every few hours on conference calls with the FEMA administrator, Craig Fugate; Secretary for Homeland Security Janet Napolitano (JNAP); John Brennan, who at the time was deputy national security adviser for homeland security and counterintelligence to the president; and me. We would update POTUS on what phase of the storm we were dealing with, how many people were without power, how many homes had flooded, what stage of response we were entering, and our latest communication with local officials. As Fugate, JNAP, and John realized how I was approaching this—with email updates to senior staff every few hours (when people know they're getting regular updates, they don't send you random questions constantly, and you can actually focus on what needs to get done in the interim) and thorough regular contact with state and local agencies—they started having me run the calls, which gave me a lot of confidence. They were trusting me with the process.

The thing you realize when you're dealing with something like this is that there is a very fine line between too many hands and not enough. I concentrated on listening to local officials, taking seriously what they were asking for and what they said they needed. It was very hard to make decisions that were impactful and responsive but not overly emotional. Listening to people describe what was happening to them, their homes—you want to wave a wand and fix it all. But there are so many stories and so many people—you have to stay focused.

I primarily dealt with the governor's offices in New York and New Jersey. I must say this: Governor Chris Christie's office was pure professionalism. I loved working with them. They were always very clear about what they needed, and they wanted us to add local mayors on the calls with the president so they could tell him what was happening in their communities directly. Fugate, JNAP, Valerie Jarrett, Cecilia

Muñoz (head of the president's Domestic Policy Council), and I all joined these calls. They were extremely productive and helped us understand where we needed to prioritize our response.

New York was not quite the same. The governor's office wanted to funnel all local communication through them, and I thought that could be bad. Local elected officials are on the front lines during a crisis, and being able to tell their constituents that they spoke directly to the president is very comforting and reassuring. People in disaster situations often don't have power or TV or Internet, so hearing their county executive on the radio saying they spoke to the president makes them feel like they are being taken care of. Also, in a state like New York, if you were in Long Island or Queens or Brooklyn, wouldn't you assume that Manhattan would be the priority for all the resources? The borough presidents should be the ones to tell POTUS about the flooding in Red Hook, Brooklyn, that had wiped out more local businesses than they could count, or the brutal scene unfolding in Breezy Point, Queens, where a six-alarm fire had burned 130 homes to the ground. I really felt the president needed to hear from the borough presidents and county executives.

So I went rogue. We added the local elected officials to the conference call ourselves and only told the governor's office at the last minute. The worst that could happen was that the governor would be pissed. After he heard the updates, and the gratitude, from the local teams, I don't think he was.

Thank God we did. We heard how deeply fucked the gas situation was all over New York. There were lines down the street for gas even though most of the gas stations were still closed; they were far short of the number of utility workers they needed to start restoring power. The storm was winding down, but the huge effects it would have were becoming clear. They didn't have enough cherry-picker cranes to start fixing power lines. Amtrak and New Jersey Transit would not be operating anytime soon.

I had to become a quasi expert on transportation infrastructure and refined fuel in a handful of days. We got a call together with Mike Froman and Gene Sperling from the White House Economic Team and John Porcari, the deputy secretary of transportation, and found out trains between New York and New Jersey couldn't start running until Substation 41 was fixed. Substation 41 was responsible for supplying power to the North River Tunnels, New York Penn Station, Amtrak, and New Jersey rail, and it was completely flooded. I asked why it hadn't been fixed. Because of the flooding, Amtrak needed divers to go and check it out, but there was some issue with their divers and they hadn't gone down yet. I asked if the Army Corps had divers. Turns out they did. I asked why they couldn't go. They could! So we sent them. And the trains (slowly) started running again.

We had a meeting in the Situation Room with the departments of Energy, Transportation, Interior, Homeland Security, and Defense. People looked tired; we had been eating a lot of grilled cheese and all looked in need of a proper salad. A lot of puffy vests and fleeces. There are a few couches in the West Wing, but no one was napping; we were all still running on adrenaline. We were trying to think of all the things we might not have been thinking about—always a good thing. I had an idea, but it seemed so small that I was nervous to blurt it out. *Are we running any PSAs with information on how to contact FEMA for assistance?*

For some people (like me), gathering the courage to speak up in meetings is a skill that requires practice. There are always the normal fears—that you'll sound stupid, that everyone else has already thought of what you're about to say and has moved on, that what you thought was a foolproof plan will have an obvious hole in it. And then there are the fears that you develop when your meetings are with the most important and powerful policy makers in the country. (They're actually pretty similar, but these meetings have added stakes: If your idea is bad, millions of people could see the consequences.)

Also, I didn't ever pontificate. I liked to know there was a real purpose behind what I was going to say. After going back and forth with myself a little bit—mostly because it seemed so basic that I assumed someone might respond, "Duh, of course we did that"—I decided to bring it up.

Everyone was like, "Wow, yes, we should do a PSA"—not a dumb idea at all. Within a few hours we had the first lady record it, commissioned an electronic billboard in Times Square to broadcast information about how to get help, and got all the hotels in the area to use the electronic screens in their lobbies (where they normally post what kinds of conventions or meetings are happening) to telegraph the information as well.

Over the course of the next 48-hour marathon, we continued to take in information and generate updates, talking with the agencies and delegating follow-up on certain issues. During this time, there was not a single phone call or email that went unanswered for more than a few minutes. It was a full cross-government effort. When we scheduled a conference call for 11:00 PM, everyone was right on time.

Soon, a crisis arose. We had bought millions of barrels of refined fuel only to realize we needed to figure out how to deliver them. There were countless calls and meetings dedicated to coming up with loopholes or ways to amend treaties to allow barges with foreign fuel into New York Harbor, and then we had to get it off the barges and into the gas stations. We eventually sent C-17s—military transport aircraft—to California to bring more trucks and utility equipment to the East Coast to transport the fuel. After that we found out most gas stations didn't have generators, which means they couldn't actually accept the fuel we had bought and transported to fill the cars that were lining the roads and highways. Quickly, state and local officials determined which gas stations served the most people and they got them generators until power was more widely restored. We were either going to be heroes or I was going to get fired.

I went to Rockaway, Queens, with Craig Fugate. Fugate is one of the most impressive people I worked with during my time at the White House. Always calm, smarter than I thought possible, philosophical, humanitarian, a logistician and educator, and just really great. We heard from local clergy that people were getting scared at night because it was so dark—most places still didn't have electricity—and there was a lot of low-grade crime, mostly looting. Fugate called New York–based production companies and got the giant lights they use to film in the dark delivered to Queens. Then we heard that people were being given the runaround by insurance companies—people who had flood insurance were being told it didn't matter because the damage to their homes had been done by wind, not water. Fugate got on the phone with the biggest providers in the area to make it clear that this was not the time for added hurdles. We also heard that many people were worried about going to FEMA for help because they thought they could get tagged for back taxes, parking tickets, or other things they simply couldn't afford to pay. We sent FEMA Corps, a trained group of volunteers, door to door with iPads to help people sign up for assistance and answer all their questions.

On our way back to DC, I asked Fugate why no one seemed to be taking from the pile of clothing donations I had seen at a Red Cross location. He explained to me the survivor-versus-victim mentality: If you had lost everything and were told you could dress yourself in hand-me-down jeans and shirts that didn't fit, would that make you feel empowered, more in control? No. A $75 gift card can be much more helpful in propelling someone forward. So when corporations asked what they could donate, he was not shy about asking for gift cards.

As people slowly started getting back on their feet and communities began to function again, we sent Cabinet secretaries to affected areas to assess the state of recovery. We deployed the small business administrator, Karen Mills, to Brooklyn,

Lower Manhattan, Westchester, and Connecticut to understand what businesses needed to reopen; she also told people about the benefits of our Disaster Loan Program, which offers financial assistance to homeowners, small business owners, and small agricultural cooperatives in declared disaster areas. Kathleen Sebelius, the secretary of health and human services, visited the hospitals in Manhattan that had lost power during the storm and thanked their staffs for their hard work. Secretary Shaun Donovan from the Department of Housing and Urban Development went to talk to people in the Bronx and Queens about what housing options were available to them. Secretary of Energy Steven Chu and Deputy Secretary of Energy Daniel Poneman convened a meeting of private and public utility companies from across the country and determined a way for them to work as a unit in times of natural disaster; they also established a 24/7 ops center at the Department of Energy. Pretty good stuff. For every visit, there was local press coverage that got out the information we knew people needed. Slowly but surely, we were seeing more calm.

Two days before the election, a nor'easter was forecast for the New York metro area. Bruce Springsteen and Jay Z were hitting the road with the president for final Get Out the Vote events. My love for Bruce Springsteen is second only to my love for the Grateful Dead, but I was in DC monitoring the storm, still resolving Sandy issues, and working with the Cabinet on their trips to damaged areas. I was very disappointed to be missing the events, but I knew my place was in the office, blasting "Land of Hope and Dreams" after everyone else had gone home.

On one of these nights, I was sitting at my desk and the phone rang. The caller ID showed that it was Jack Lew, the White House chief of staff. We had done a storm update about an hour or so earlier, so I didn't know why he was calling. When people are traveling with POTUS, they often call because something has gone wrong and they want to air their frustrations on the unsuspecting person on the other line. "Who thought this was a good idea?" etc. I really wasn't in the mood for whatever the issue might be. Also, I had been seeing the pictures on TV all day, and I didn't want a pity "What's going on in the office? I'm trying to sound like I'm not having the time of my life!" call. I answered with a listless, slightly cranky, "Hey."

But it wasn't Jack on the line. A voice said, "Alyssa?"

OH MY GOD. I knew the voice.

He didn't immediately say, "It's Bruce Springsteen," but he sounds just like his music—it was like a saxophone could come in at any minute. He thanked me for my work on Hurricane Sandy on behalf of the people of New Jersey.

Because I am a real tool, I was so shocked and flustered that I told him he probably had better things to be doing on Air Force One than talking to me. I said I appreciated his call, and then we hung up.

On Election Day, I walked down to the AME church on 15th Street to vote. I talked to Rahm Emmanuel while I was waiting and called Secretary Donovan to give him a heads-up that I had suggested to the president that he be named head of the Sandy Recovery Task Force and that POTUS might be calling him shortly—sorry, not sorry.

ALYSSA MASTROMONACO

Me and my Omie in our fabulous coats. I have binoculars because she loved to look at birds.

CLAY DUMAS

Me channeling my inner Diane Keaton in preparation for my interview with Charlie Rose.

PETE SOUZA

Before "Alyssa and Kathy's Last-Chance Dance," the White House threw us a cocktail party to celebrate our last day. This is the Oval Office back patio; that's Kathy talking to POTUS.

PETE SOUZA

The entire scheduling and advance team freaking out on election night at Grant Park. I went home early to get some sleep, so I'm not in this photo, but the guy in flip-flops is having enough fun for the both of us.

The coolest I've ever looked, on Marine One across from POTUS.

ARUN CHAUDHARY

Marv and me on NightHawk 2 on our way to see the launch of Space Shuttle *Endeavour* on April 29, 2011. It was canceled due to an equipment problem, but I got another slick sunglasses photo out of it.

This is the reception for Plouffe's last day. I'm telling a very funny story.

White House Chief of Staff Bill Daley once told me he would like to "burn those pants" and that they looked like something Rodney Dangerfield would wear. I loved them.

POTUS, WH Chief of Staff Denis McDonough, me, and Deputy Chief of Staff for Policy Rob Nabors in the Oval. Denis looks good.

Me resisting POTUS's attempts to antagonize me with my thirty-sixth birthday gift. (It was a really beautiful rose gold bracelet.)

PETE SOUZA

Everyone breathlessly anticipating whether I will poop on the pope.

PETE SOUZA

Pfeiffer, POTUS, and White House Press Secretary Jay Carney told me I was the size of a hedgehog, so I was pretending to be a hedgehog.

PETE SOUZA

In the middle of our 2009 trip to Iraq, we had to change plans midflight because a sandstorm was rolling through. This is the conference room on Air Force One; I had secret plastic bags in my jacket pockets in case I needed to puke on the helicopter.

POTUS drops in on me, Joe Paulsen, and Bobby Schmuck having a meeting in my office. Note my zip-up fashion hoodie.

PETE SOUZA

Me, POTUS, and Deputy Chief of Staff for Policy Mona Sutphen on our way back from Ghana.

PETE SOUZA

My sister and me with POTUS in New York. I routinely wore sequins to work.

Smoot and me outlining our plans for a fund-raiser at Paris Fashion Week in 2012: Kanye West would be there, and I was going to get to the bottom of whether he was really dating Kim Kardashian.

POTUS receives an update on Hurricane Sandy at FEMA headquarters. FEMA Administrator Craig Fugate is on the right.

Messing around on Marine One with FLOTUS (who looks great), FLOTUS's Chief of Staff Tina Tchen, and Jay Carney.

PETE SOUZA

"Do you like the debt ceiling? Check box Y/N."

PETE SOUZA

Marv, VPOTUS, my messy desk, and what is possibly an issue of *People* magazine.

Me, Plouffe, and Favs on the campaign trail in summer 2012, trying to figure out if the diner across the street is open.

JASON REED/REUTERS

November 22, 2013: me, DK, and Supreme Court Justice Elena Kagan picking out our wedding vows in her office. The bride wore Stella McCartney in petrol blue.

While the job would be hugely satisfying in many ways, the months after a disaster are also when people start to become annoyed that things are taking so long.

That night, Anita Decker Breckenridge, the personal aide to the president, and I went to BLT Steak for a (very) early-bird dinner. We had a few fall-inspired cocktails and shared a steak. I was asleep by 10:30 PM and never saw POTUS's election night speech. It was clear he would win, and the beauty of YouTube is that I knew I could watch the speech the next day—all I wanted to do was lay my head down on the pillow. Maybe this sounds anticlimactic, but I really thought we were going to win, and it was nice to have a moment of rest. A lot of the dudes wanted to be out in Chicago to bask with POTUS, but I didn't feel like my part in the campaign wasn't going to be acknowledged just because I wasn't there.

* * *

A few weeks later, the *New York Times* printed a story about the White House staff in which someone made an offhand comment about the scope of my job. The article was about the selection process for Obama's new chief of staff, and I got a passing mention: "Alyssa Mastromonaco, relatively young at 36, has managed Mr. Obama's logistical and travel arrangements since he first started running for president six years ago, and will remain as deputy chief of staff for operations, responsible for overseeing scheduling, personnel and much more."

No big deal, right? I went apeshit. After all I'd been through that election cycle, whoever had talked to this reporter had characterized my job as "basically a travel agent." I had always been very sensitive about this idea that I only handled "travel and logistics"; I also felt that, if someone had been describing what Jim Messina had done in my position, they would have said he ran the White House.

I don't want to blame my reaction on fatigue, but it didn't help. The press office had circulated the story to senior advisers, and as soon as I read it, I replied-all with a very cutting, infuriated response. I thought it was totally warranted. In a show of solidarity, Kathy Ruemmler, the White House Counsel, my dear friend, and the woman who, at 35, delivered the closing arguments in the Enron case, also replied-all and echoed my sentiment, saying she agreed with me. It was extremely disappointing, we said, that we weren't having each other's backs. You don't talk about your colleagues on background, and you definitely don't on-the-record them. If a reporter approached you, it was understood that you would flag it for comms.

After that, I let it go; I was fuming, but I didn't think it was a big deal—sometimes you just have to say what you want to say. I figured people would read my email, maybe whoever said what they said to the *Times* would feel bad, and that would be enough.

The next morning I came in for the 7:30 senior advisers meeting, and Clay told me that POTUS wanted to see me.

Walking to his office, I had no idea what he would want to talk about, but being called down to the office rarely meant anything bad. I wasn't nervous, so I just went in.

"So," he said, "I hear you sent quite an email."

I was totally taken aback. How the hell did he know about

the email? I instantly started going over that distribution list in my head to figure out who had narc'd on me.

I wear every thought on my face; POTUS knew immediately that I was mentally rating each person on my team on a scale from innocent to "deserves another irrational email." "It doesn't matter who came to talk to me," he said. He went on to say that I needed to realize the power of my words. I could not send emails like that because they—I am paraphrasing—freak everyone out.

Developing self-awareness is a lifelong process; you don't just wake up one day and have all you need. So even though I'd spent the last few months demonstrating that I was capable and knew what I was doing, this was something of a revelation. When the president of the United States tells you your words are powerful, it can be pretty shocking. I honestly didn't think anyone would give a shit if I sent a snippy email.

It was good advice, specifically to me at the time but generally as it relates to any kind of replying-all in life: Think about how what you say could affect people, from the top down. It was also a wake-up call for me about my state of mind: I didn't know why (yet)—though I'm sure I did, deep down—but my temper was getting worse, and my fuse shorter and shorter.

CHAPTER 5

Some Personal Shit You Should Probably Know

Sometime in early August of that year, Plouffe was in my office and we were shooting the shit. Since I am a master typist, I was looking at him, talking, and typing an email at the same time, which I might have done on any given day. But as he was leaving, he got this worried look on his face. He furrowed his brow in a very classic Plouffe expression and asked, "What are you doing?"

I looked at the computer. Nothing I had typed made sense. It wasn't even words.

I had been losing things lately. I had misplaced my keys. I would get in the car and not remember if I had fed my cat, Shrummie. I had misplaced my beloved binder more than once; I had even left it at home one day, which I had never done before in my life. Earlier that summer I forgot that I had already put my NuvaRing in, put a second one in, and didn't realize until I got my period and two Nuvas popped out. (Luckily that explained the historic adult acne I had developed that month.) When I saw the nonsense on my screen, all this

124

came together, and I panicked. I was convinced I had a brain tumor. I also, apparently, didn't realize I had started talking to myself, because after Plouffe walked out, my assistant, Brundage, heard me talking—saying what, I don't know—and called the White House Medical Unit. He told them I was on my way and sent me over. I walked past the Rose Garden and down the Colonnade fighting back tears.

Working in the White House is incredible, but it is also completely, totally exhausting—and exhausting isn't even descriptive enough. You set your alarm for 5:00 AM and wake up only to assess the state of your hair; "It looks fine," you decide, and go back to sleep until 5:15. You wake up at 5:15 and negotiate with yourself that "fresh faces are beautiful," to get in that second tranche of 15 minutes. Working for the president got me to stop wearing makeup altogether; it's becoming popular now, but back then you would come in with nothing on and everyone would ask if you were sick. You told yourself the dark circles made you look like an operative working in the Green Zone, even though you really lived in Georgetown with a nice man and a Persian cat.

The absolute best part is the White House Med Unit. Doc Jackson calmed me down and gave me a complete neurological exam. I was so panicked I don't remember much of it, but I think he tested my reflexes and coordination, and I walked back and forth a few times. He concluded that due to extreme exhaustion caused by lack of sleep, I was operating at about 50 percent of my capacity. I agreed I would go to sleep—not just be in bed, but, like, snoozing—by 10:00 PM and take Ambien for a few weeks. It was the first time that I admitted to myself that I might not make it two full terms.

I first talked to POTUS about possibly leaving the White House a couple of months later, shortly after his reelection. We were on AF1 on our way back from a trip to Asia. I wasn't certain I wanted to leave right at that very moment, but I felt it coming, and for all the opportunities Barack Obama had given me, I felt like I should let him know what I was thinking. It wasn't easy; I didn't want to seem like a wimp for opting out, and also, once you say something like that, you can't really take it back. He told me he believed I just needed a vacation and that I should take one; he didn't sound disappointed or judgmental. I agreed to take a break around the holidays.

Unfortunately, that break didn't come. The person I thought would travel as acting chief of staff couldn't go to Hawaii with the first family, so I had to go. We thought this would be an easy year, for once, but the White House and Congress were still heavily negotiating the ability to raise the debt ceiling—if it wasn't raised, it would have been cataclysmic for the economy and our standing globally. We were also in the middle of nominating a new secretary of defense. I had to go.

Here is your opportunity to roll your eyes at my being sad about spending Christmas in Hawaii. I get it. I always try to be present and aware of my situation and surroundings; when I spiral into self-pity, I know there are people far worse off than I am. In general, I probably suffer from what my friend Anne would call "uptown problems"; these have also been called "first-world problems" and "privilege," but no matter which term you use, it means the same thing: It's not that bad.

But I was totally spent, and I felt incapable of working any more. I also really, really love Christmas. The German side of my family instilled in us early on the importance of a grand spread with many types of meats and cheeses and cake. It would be the first year—ever—that I wasn't with my family. Even during the campaign in 2008, I flew home for Christmas Eve dinner and went back to Chicago on Christmas Day. I was almost devastated about having to go to Hawaii, though Nancy-Ann DeParle, the deputy chief of staff for policy, did get me an amazing sweater with a cat on it that I was really looking forward to wearing on the plane.

We were leaving on a Friday. I had been dating the nice man in Georgetown, David, for a little more than two years, and since we would be spending the holidays apart, we decided to go to our spot, Cafe Milano, for a preholiday dinner on Thursday night. David was chief of staff to Senate Majority Leader Harry Reid from Nevada, so it wasn't particularly upsetting that we weren't going to be together—he would have to work anyway.

I was late, it was pouring rain, and we sat down next to the loudest people I've ever encountered. By the time my food came, I was laughing, because nothing was going right and we didn't get a chance to say basically anything to each other the entire time.

We finished eating, and David asked if I wanted dessert. If anyone ever asks you if you want dessert in a restaurant, something is up. Who orders dessert in a restaurant? Unless it's a special occasion or they need more time to tell you something bad, no one orders dessert in a restaurant. I remember saying very clearly, "No, I just want to go home and take my Spanx off." (Update: I have not worn Spanx since leaving the White House.) We walked outside.

Down the street from Cafe Milano there is a little brick building that contains a Domino's Pizza. In front of this Domino's Pizza, in the rain, David asked me to marry him.

David had three rules in life, and he would often recite them, I thought, to make it clear that we would never get married. The rules were: (1) rent, don't own; (2) no pets; and (3) never get married. I never harbored those romantic-comedy illusions that I would be the one to change him; I was totally shocked. First by the proposal, and then by the giant ring.

We walked home (still raining), and I called my family. David's phone rang. It was Jack Lew and Rob Nabors to talk about the debt ceiling. He got on the phone with them, told them we had just gotten engaged, I heard a "Mazel tov!" through the phone from Jack, and then they talked about the debt ceiling.

I emailed Pfeiffer to tell him, and he wrote back saying he had read my email as "I got enraged" before he realized it said "engaged."

The next day, I left for Hawaii. We were announcing that John Kerry would be the next secretary of state, so he was in the West Wing when we met before the trip. He and Mrs. Heinz—also our neighbors in Georgetown—were so pleased to hear about my engagement. The vice president came in for hugs. Tina Tchen, the first lady's chief of staff, got misty-eyed. VJ, too. And there were Dey, Jess, and the whole SkedAdv gang. On AF1 a few hours later, the first lady insisted on seeing my ring and having a glass of champagne to kick off the trip. When we landed, I found my room had been decorated for Christmas by the advance team, complete with a small tree and lights.

I was feeling a lot better; I don't like attention, so the whole celebration made me uncomfortable, but I also felt so loved. In my euphoria—and impending jet lag—I decided that my second stop at the Westin Moana Surfrider should be to get my nails done. If I was going to be showing off my ring finger, it should at least have tame cuticles! I didn't look at the prices and ended up spending $400 on a really boring Ballet Slippers mani-pedi.

I had a mai tai with Eric Schultz, the White House associate communications director, and went to bed. We had a daily call about Chuck Hagel and his nomination for secretary of defense, and it was at 4:00 AM Hawaii time.

That is working at the White House in a nutshell: For every glamorous state dinner, every surreal conversation about '80s music with a foreign dignitary, every glass of champagne on Air Force One, there is a 4:00 AM conference call. The advent of BlackBerries and the 24/7 news cycle—neither of which was really around when I first got into government—ensures almost no meaningful rest. My hair had turned completely white from stress. That's just how it is. You kind of know what you're getting into when you start, but you also have no idea what it will really be like.

If one of my goals in writing this book is to get more women interested in and excited about working in government, then this is the part where it starts to get difficult, because I have to be honest about what it's like to work in government. For me, anyway.

At any high-powered job, you're going to have to work a lot. America is a nation of people who work a lot and of people who strive to work a lot. The best thing you can be, our culture tells us, is "at the top of your field." You are supposed to want to have power, to be an executive with a cushy corner office and a lot of money and an assistant, a person who travels for business and takes working breakfasts, fork in one hand and cell phone in the other. When I worked at the White House, this was my life, minus the corner office and the large quantity of money, but with the added bonus of being able to do something I really loved for causes that I really believed in, with people who taught me something new every day, if not every hour. Saying you love working for a politician often makes you seem like a shill, or full of shit, but I truly loved working for Barack Obama, and I think he's one of a few politicians for whom that kind of statement is believable. I loved being a part of an administration that I thought was making the country better, and I had an incredibly generous, kind, and helpful boss who I felt had not only *my* best interests at heart but also the entire nation's. Plus, when I traveled for work, I took Air Force One, which never got old, and instead of wasting time at boring conference centers I was doing things like eating goat in the courtyard of Hamid Karzai's palace. They wouldn't let me inside because I was a woman and they didn't believe I was actually part of the senior staff that was cleared to go in, but still: Not much is cooler.

So for a long time I worked at my capacity, or over my capacity. It didn't really matter—I was young, and I was happy to do it. I had never imagined I would make it to where I did, especially not as soon as I did, so I felt like I had to do whatever it took to make sure the faith POTUS—and Pete Rouse, and Plouffe, and all these other people—had in me was not misplaced. I always found this to be extremely rewarding. To be able to prove to yourself that you can work more, and at a higher level, than you ever would have thought possible is motivating in itself. Truly believing in what you're doing helps.

But when I was promoted to deputy chief in January 2011, a lot about "my personal life"—which bled into my work life, as it often does at jobs that maintain even just normal hours—had to change. In my first month as deputy chief, the Egyptian president, Hosni Mubarak, was deposed. That day was also Gibbs's last in the White House, and I couldn't go to the good-bye karaoke party until we got a group of American citizens ("AmCits" in national security speak) out of Cairo.

After that, I pretty much stopped going out with people from work, or really going out at all. David and I were dating by this point, but we weren't that serious; we went out twice a week, usually to this Chinese restaurant in Dupont Circle, Meiwah, on Wednesdays and to somewhere fancier on Saturdays, until we got engaged. I didn't make other plans because I got to work at around 6:45 in the morning and just wanted silence when I left by 8:00 PM; I also didn't want to have to cancel on people if something came up. I didn't necessarily have a ton of STUFF to do, but I always could have had something to do, at any moment of any day. So when I wasn't in the office, I stayed in my apartment, waiting. I had two secure phones—the top secret phone, for really-not-good matters, was red—and a secure computer in my bedroom. They made it extremely warm.

I never felt like I was missing out. The pressure made me grow and learn and all that good stuff, and although my old job, as director of scheduling and advance, was much more fun, my new job meant that my colleagues began to see me in a different way. Even Dey, who had been with me basically since the beginning of my time with Obama, reported to me differently. People stop seeing your interactions with them as playful banter; they start getting serious around you. The tenor of respect shifts. It's not worse or better—but it is different.

It was also difficult to have friends, or date, with so much responsibility. For one thing, I had had a very personal relationship with POTUS for many years; people would always ask me things like "Did he really quit smoking?" or "Who came to his birthday party?" as well as questions about insider government information, and I couldn't answer any of them and maintain his trust. (I had also taken an oath.) When I did go out, I didn't really drink, because I was afraid I'd say something I shouldn't. I had a roster of stories that I would tell at parties that weren't with White House people—though I rarely went to those—and I wouldn't go beyond that. At my first White House press dinner, I didn't drink at all. There were hundreds of reporters in a room— you have two glasses of wine and tell a funny story and then all of a sudden you're a "reliable source." It was the loneliest time of my life.

When I started to wear down, I didn't really know what to do. Most people leave the White House after about three years because it's so draining, but I felt this emotional, personal connection to everyone there—we all did—and I didn't want to let them down. It's also strange to have such a weighty job when you're really young—it's hard to imagine what you'll do afterward. You have a skill set, experiences, and knowledge that very few people can also say they have. You feel like you can do anything but also like there's nothing else you can do. Meanwhile, the stress is taking its toll on you—physically, emotionally, everything.

. . .

When I turned 35, Reggie Love came up to me in the Navy Mess. "Boss, happy birthday!" he said. He doesn't forget a birthday. "Did you know that, according to CNN, you are of advanced maternal age?"

Reggie and I had been working together since he started as a Senate intern in 2005—we were tight. This was a weird thing for him to say, and I was a little...surprised...but it was fine. (After all, it was true.) All the junior staff people in the Mess were shocked; I had to tell them it was OK to laugh.

At panels for women in government or women in media or any other type of panel that I might be on (it's usually about getting more women represented somewhere), I'm always asked about children. Do I feel like I sacrificed having kids to pursue my career? Was it hard to make that choice? What do my parents think? And when people finally seem to have exhausted this invasive line of questioning, they add, "Are you sure?" As a childless 40-year-old woman, I am either supposed to regret not having kids or be entrenched in the expensive and often disappointing process of IVF.

I wish that our culture didn't demand women have an opinion on this. You don't have to have an opinion on it. I always respond to the questions with something very diplomatic: I am not a victim, I say. Having kids is one way of being happy, but I too am very happy, and well adjusted; I like my house and my husband and my cats and my job. I have time to mentor young women and to see my parents. Many of my friends around my age also don't have children, and none of them are super bummed about it. I'm a godmother. And I do really love my cats. This is sometimes seen as sad, or cat-lady-ish, but I think that is sexist. (Let's remember Hemingway—dude had a lot of cats.) Oprah also doesn't have kids, and she is doing just fine; she gets to hang out with kids all the time—and then she gets to go home to Stedman and they go on a lavish vacation.

I truly believe all this. It is not some story I concocted late at night trying to rationalize the fact that I spent my peak childbearing years meeting foreign dignitaries and helping the United States respond to natural disasters.

But there is something else—something I don't tell the well-meaning people who ask me what it's like to be a childless 40-year-old woman with a successful career. I always regret not talking about it, because I don't think enough people talk about things like this, but it seems like too much information. The fact is, in addition to having always put my career first and not getting married until I was 37, getting pregnant is just not an option for me.

My period was always fucked up, for my whole life. When I was a teenager, my hormones turned me into a menace; when I finally went on birth control when I was 23 or 24, it was because I couldn't stop sweating—I would ruin shirts—and my doctor recommended a low-estrogen pill. I always got nauseated with the pill, but my gynecologist didn't believe me; this went on for a while, until I finally started using the NuvaRing, which I loved, for about ten years. So many women have a birth control saga like this—it sucks.

Even with the sweating, all this birth control would suggest that I thought I was capable of getting pregnant, which I did. But a few months after Reggie wished me a very biological birthday, I went to the doctor and asked him if he would give me an AMH—or Anti-Mullerian Hormone—test. An AMH test measures what is referred to as "ovarian reserve," a phrase I have always thought was very funny; in normal-person terms, it measures how many eggs you have left. (Actually, it measures the amount of AMH present in your blood, which is a reflection of how many eggs you have left.) It's not common to give an AMH test to someone who is 35 and not actively trying to conceive—I had to beg my doctor to do it.

I got the idea to take the test from the Internet. DK and I had just started dating, and although we weren't anywhere close to having a discussion about kids, I was personally curious. I had started doing the math in my head—"Well, we'd have to be dating for at least a year, and by that time I'll be 36…"—and I wanted to know if I even had time to roll the dice.

AMH tests are scaled from 0 to 7, where 0 is probably no eggs, 1.5 to 4.0 is normal, and anything above 4 is high, which often suggests you have polycystic ovary syndrome (PCOS). I clocked in at 0.2, which is the AMH level of a woman who is about 60 years old.

It was not *devastating*, but it was shocking. It was so final—from that moment on, I didn't have to wonder if I would ever have kids, because I knew I would not be having them, at least not with my own eggs. I didn't want to dwell on the missed opportunity when there are so many other ways to create a family; adopting is not off the table, but it's not something I thought about that much then. I didn't cry, and I don't remember telling my parents.

If the test had come back as a 1.5, I might have been sadder, because it would have meant I had to make a decision. The finality of that barely-there number took the pressure off. I couldn't even think that it was unfair, because I knew that I was older and sometimes things just don't work out. What I did think about was the fact that I would forever be looked at funny by other people, who, deep down, probably pity me for not having kids. That was the truly sad part.

The world has a funny way of driving home a point. Around the same time that I found out about my "ovarian reserve," I went to a dinner South Korea hosted for the White House in Seoul. The setup was not conducive to chitchat; we were seated at one long, King Arthur–ish table, and I was two or three seats down from Lee Myung-bak, the president of Korea, and across from Pfeiffer. I was the only woman, which made Pfeiffer laugh, because no one was talking to me.

Because I always prepared a lot for state dinners, I knew that the person next to me—it might have been the treasury secretary—had three kids, two sons and a daughter, so I started asking him about his family. He lit up; he was super pumped to talk about his kids.

After a while, though, I noticed he hadn't said anything about his daughter, so I asked about her as well. He replied that, because his daughter was 30 and unmarried, "As you would say in America, she is an 'old maid.'" I discreetly moved a ring I was wearing to the significant finger and finished the dinner without incident.

CHAPTER 6

Confidence, or
The Hope Flood

I met David the same way I met the serious boyfriend I had before him, Marv, whom I'd broken up with about five years before: work.

Some people may think this is tragic. It's not! Besides, both are extremely cute stories; Marv and I met when I was staff assistant to the press and scheduling office for Senator Kerry; he was an intern in the DC office, and we had to fax things back and forth, which led to email flirting, which led to dating. And yet there's still no movie called *You've Got a Fax*.

The story with David is a little more technologically advanced. It was late 2009, we'd been in office for a little under a year, and my boss, Jim Messina, was working on a project in Nevada called CityCenter. It involved Senator Harry Reid, so Jim introduced me to Senator Reid's chief of staff, David, over email so we could work on getting POTUS involved. Jim said something like, "He's so cool, he only dates women who live in California, and he has a Porsche." OK. Not the best impression to go in with.

DK and I started emailing about the project, and it was kind of flirty, but nothing overt. I was looking forward to eventually getting to meet him in person, but for no real, concrete reason. Sometimes you can be talking to someone and you just feel it.

Then, on Christmas Day, a man tried to detonate a plastic bomb he'd hidden in his underwear on a flight to Detroit. I called David and said I didn't think it was the right time for POTUS to get involved with the project—it didn't really make sense to send the president to the opening of a mall at that point—and that we should put it on hold until the new year.

In the meantime, we emailed about the project off and on, and we talked about other things. I made some *Saved by the Bell* jokes and was impressed that he got them. Things were shaping up.

Then, about two weeks after POTUS came back to the White House at the beginning of January, a magnitude 7.0 earthquake hit Haiti about 15 miles west of its capital.

It was completely catastrophic. When the White House got news of the disaster, POTUS coordinated a relief effort pretty much immediately. According to the ticktock, the minute-by-minute outline of an event that the White House comms team would send out afterward, POTUS heard about the quake at 5:52 PM in the Oval Office on January 12, and by 9:00 PM he was in the Situation Room for an emergency meeting to figure out the relief effort, which would include the deployment of thousands of troops and $100 million in aid. He asked a small group of people to go to Haiti to coordinate it immediately: Tommy Vietor, the National Security spokesperson; Denis McDonough, a senior national security adviser; and me.

I didn't think twice about agreeing to go, but as soon as I did, I was scared out of my mind. I couldn't believe I said I would do this; I had no idea what to expect, except that it would be very, very hard.

As part of my preparation to go, I emailed David and told him I was going away and that he should contact Danielle if anything came up with the CityCenter project.

He asked where I was going, and I said Haiti.

He replied, "You have to come back safe so I can take you out to dinner."

!!!

I knew we had been flirting. I was reasonably sure. But when I opened that email—and you're always sort of nervous to get emails from people you want to get emails from, even in normal situations when you're not about to head into a disaster area—I moved back from the computer. We had never met in person. We had spoken on the phone only once.

I thought the team and I would fly to Haiti in a jet, but when I showed up at the White House on the day we were supposed to leave, I realized we would be going in a C-17—an Army cargo plane. When something this devastating happens, everything you take for granted in a normal situation—roads, running water, the airport—has stopped functioning, and we couldn't get there any other way. I had told Tommy not to worry about supplies, so I showed up at this cargo plane, which was full of Marines, with a bunch of Whole Foods bags filled with beef jerky and granola bars.

We were wearing corduroys and Patagonia fleeces. "We look like Joanie and Chachi!" I hissed at Tommy as we got out of the car at Langley Air Force Base. We were terrified.

When we got off the plane, it was very dark; most places didn't have electricity, but for the entire time we were there we worked out of airport hangars, which had some. My job was to coordinate transportation and other logistics, but there was just no way to get anywhere—and we had to figure out how to make it to the embassy. We eventually got a ride from someone who worked at the airport. After that, for the five or six days we were there, we hitchhiked everywhere we went. Before I left, Ferial was really worried, and she gave me about 30 packages of gum to use to barter in case of an emergency; I thought she was crazy until I figured out I could pay people to drive me around in packs of gum.

Everyone who was part of the relief effort—a lot of people—slept side by side in sleeping bags in the embassy, and no one showered for a week. For food, we had my bougie snacks and MREs, or Meals, Ready-to-Eat, which are field rations the military gives to soldiers in combat and other areas where food isn't readily available. As you know, I have IBS, so these almost immediately gave me diarrhea, a condition that is especially not good when you have to share a toilet with 75 other people and can't bathe.

This is when I started drinking red wine seriously. It helps with stomach problems, and when Captain John Kirby, our guide in Haiti, who went on to become the spokesperson for the State Department, heard I was not doing well, he introduced me to the guys who controlled the embassy's special-occasion stash. After that, every night we would get a juice cup of red wine with our MREs, and we would go sit on our sleeping bags to have our dinner. Now I associate red wine with community and generosity—a strong contrast to what was otherwise a sad, hard time. Much of what we were doing when we were working out of airports was helping people find their families and repatriating bodies. At one point, David texted me to make sure I got there OK, but I wasn't thinking about that at all anymore.

After a week, we came back on another cargo plane through Tampa, got burgers at Applebee's, and then transferred, still unshowered, to a commercial flight to DC. Once we landed there, we went to our respective apartments and crashed.

■ ■ ■

The next day, I showed up at work to find an envelope on my desk. I was still exhausted and dazed to be back, but the contents would have been a shock even if my mind had been in a more normal place. It was a pair of gift certificates for me and a friend to go to dinner and the spa at the Four Seasons. From David.

!!!

A man had never even bought me a drink in a bar before. How that's possible, I don't really know. Maybe it was the fact that I looked like a fifth-grade boy in my early-to-mid-twenties, when women are most likely to be bought drinks in bars. Maybe it's that the suave banker with good cheekbones swooping in and asking the bartender to put it on his tab is a myth perpetuated by romantic comedies, and it doesn't happen that often anyway. Maybe it's that I lived by Mo Mannino's favorite saying in the Rhinebeck High School yearbook: "Everyone has an angle." And he didn't mean it in the *America's Next Top Model* kind of way—he meant it like "Trust no one." Once you internalize that, it's hard not to be skeptical of random men when they come within 10 feet.

Whenever I did try to let loose and flirt with strangers, it always backfired. After college, when I was sharing a room with her in side-by-side twin beds, Volpes had her birthday party at Polly Esther's, a bar near Hudson Street. Polly Esther's was known as a haunt for the "bridge and tunnel crowd" and beloved—or despised—for playing music from different decades on each floor. If anyone but a very trusted friend ever invites you to a bar that plays music from different decades on each floor, beware—it demonstrates a lack of commitment. I agreed because (1) it was Volpes's birthday, and (2) I hoped for a little "Smooth Criminal" on the '80s floor. I can't say I enjoyed bars or clubs otherwise—I got little sense of possibility from them.

At Polly Esther's, Volpes and her friends from Garden City and I were dancing away when this sort of pasty group of dudes migrated toward us. Always looking out for me, Volpes advised me, in my bebe tank top and fit-and-flare pants, to go dance with them.

When I got over there, they informed me that they were Welsh paratroopers. They told me this over and over, despite the fact they were neither Welsh nor paratroopers. I learned that they were not who they claimed because one of them walked me home and gave me his number, which Volpes encouraged me to call/taunted me with the next day. When I called the number, a woman answered the phone; she was confused but definitely not of Welsh descent. I don't remember the guy's name, but I do remember that when I asked for him, the woman laughed. I then came down with the flu, which Volpes referred to as the Welsh clap.

David and I started talking on the phone. The trip to Vegas was finally scheduled for February 18, and we planned to go out to dinner on the free night I would have when I was there. I brought an outfit I thought Carrie Bradshaw would wear: cargo jacket, J.Crew sweater, pearls, jeans, high heels. In retrospect I don't know why I thought she would wear this, because it is what everyone was wearing at the time.

The big day arrives, I am jittery and excited and counting down the hours, and around 4:00 PM David calls. "Hey," he says. "I talked to Jim Messina, and he's going to join us for dinner."

What? I had been under the impression that I was being wooed, for basically the first time in my life, and then he goes and invites my boss to our long-awaited first date? Was I being tricked?

I called my friends to tell them there was no way I was going on this date anymore. It was offensive and not OK that he had invited Jim.

They told me to stop being a baby, get a vodka screwdriver, and go on the date. If I hated it, I could always leave.

When I showed up at the restaurant, sure enough, Jim Messina was there. I was fuming but charming; I got a steak. Even though I often order steak at restaurants, I felt this time it was making some kind of point. Like, "Oh, this? You thought this was a date? I just came for the steak." I believe the men had tuna.

Afterward, David walked me back to the Bellagio, where we were staying, and asked if I wanted to go out again.

"Well, that depends," I said. "Will it just be me and you, or should I bring all my girlfriends?"

From that point on we went out twice a week until we got engaged outside the Domino's in 2012. We were married at the end of 2013. (More on that in a second.) (Don't worry—it's not at all a fairy-tale kind of thing.)

▪ ▪ ▪

I always felt kind of apathetic about my love life, for the most part. People try to project things onto you when you're a single woman in her thirties, but I wasn't upset when my friends were getting engaged and married and I wasn't. I was helping run the country, in a small way, and traveling the world and spending my time with brilliant people. I came to identify fiercely with the independence all this gave me. I realize it might be a little disappointing to see a woman start off a discussion about confidence by talking about her love life, but in some ways, having David woo me was a more alien experience, one that required a lot of self-possession and confidence, than something like talking about fjords at a state dinner with Chile's minister of tourism.

Throughout my adult life, I was always pretty confident when I moved from job to job. After I had that (very) brief stint as a rubber secretary at Merrill Lynch, I grew to understand and trust my gut, but I had also learned that I acclimate pretty well, and that every job has a learning curve that you have to, ahem, lean into. Every time you change jobs, even if you're coming in as the editor in chief or senior marketing manager or whatever, you will have first-day jitters. You will still spend an hour (or two) thinking about what you should wear. Those jitters don't mean you're about to fail; they're what get you ready to dive into something headfirst.

After I became Obama's adviser/director of scheduling in late 2004, Pete Rouse became my spiritual guide and mentor. Pete had worked in Washington for about 40 years, many of those as chief of staff to the Senate majority leader, and was known as the "101st senator" and "mayor of Capitol Hill." He knew everyone and didn't like talking to any of them. Walking the halls with him always involved some commentary on the people he considered to be violating his personal space. There is no one more thoughtful in the way they give advice. He returns every email, makes every connection, and does it all while being a wheeler and dealer. His code name in the White House was "Possum," which is why from here on out he will be referred to only as Possum. Also, he loves cats.

When we got to the Senate, Possum drafted one of his famous "strategic plans"—lengthy, painfully thorough memos about how to get something done. In this case, it was the strategic plan for Senator Obama's first year, and it could be summed up as "workhorse, not show horse." It included lots of time with constituents and in Illinois, and less time with DC insiders and celebrities. Obama was quite fine with that.

Every decision we made had to stand up to the workhorse vs. show horse test.

Obama had a political action committee called the Hope Fund that was right down the street from the Hart Senate Office Building on Mass Ave. The Hope Fund ran initiatives for getting young adults from diverse backgrounds into community organizing and politics; it also managed Obama's political engagements. I had been working in the Senate office for a little more than a year when Pete decided I should replace the Hope Fund's outgoing political director, who was moving to Paris.

Initially, I was psyched. I thought "political director" was an awesome title. I would be lying if I said I really knew what the job entailed, but I trusted Possum to know what was best.

Before I was offered the job, I had been working in the back office with Favs, Tommy Vietor, Possum, and Gibbs. I loved it there. We sat near the back door of Senator Obama's office, so he would come out and visit with us a lot. Sometimes he would come to talk about policy issues; sometimes he and the guys would talk about sports. (I would chime in about gymnastics, swimming, and ice-skating during the Olympics, but that's about it.) On occasion, we might have a little squabble over Mariah Carey. (The specifics of the squabble are classified.) I think it was back there that we all really developed a bond. One night during a Voterama—what usually happens before the Senate breaks for a recess and they vote on measures late into the night to get everything done—Senator Obama came out the back door and walked in on me doing sit-ups on the floor. Most senators would have been appalled; he said, "Good for you." On Friday mornings, after a bad Thursday, Tommy and Favs and I would get French toast from the cafeteria. On Friday afternoons, the bros and I would get the $7 Maniac Special (tempura, sushi, and some teriyaki) at Kyoto.

After I reflected on all the good times we'd had in Obama's Senate office, I had a meltdown. The prospect of moving three blocks down the street to work at the Hope Fund filled me with dread.

Why? I had a lot of bad reasons. I was happy for the promotion, but it was definitely outside my comfort zone. I don't love talking to people I don't know, but this job would put me in charge of our political engagements for the 2006 midterm elections; I would also manage Obama's profile and relationships. That was a lot of responsibility, and it would be the first time I was really at the tip of the spear—this was going to be my first experience being the Boss. I did not get the impression that the Hope Fund staff were psyched I was coming down there, either. I had no reason to feel that way, but that didn't matter!

I dragged out the transition for a few weeks. Each time someone asked me why I was still in the Senate office, I had a different excuse, but I never deviated too far from "Wrapping up a few projects!" I thought I had everyone fooled—until one day, when Possum called me into his office and asked, "Why the hell are you still here?"

As soon as he asked, I started to cry. That's right. I cry a lot, but I generally think it's not OK to cry in front of your boss. If you're feeling real emotion about something that merits strong feelings, fine, but at best, you come off as "sensitive," and at worst you seem like you're trying to use your tears to get what you want. I told Possum I was afraid to leave; he told me I had one hour to pack my stuff and get to the Hope Fund office, three blocks away from $7 Maniac Fridays and all my friends.

This was NOT a big deal, but I really felt like it was. I argued that I was probably too important to leave the Senate office, that Obama needed me nearby (he didn't), and that I should probably stay. Possum told me again, loudly, to get out of there and start my new job. He was mad. I knew he had decided to move me over in part because it would benefit me—undoubtedly I would be able to grow and develop a new skill set. I was being my own worst enemy.

One of my main goals in writing this book is to give you the permission to admit to feeling or doing things that are silly; once you do, you can get on with your life. So here it is, the real reason why I didn't want to go down the street: The crew at the Hope Fund had been together since the Senate race in 2003. They were all friends, and I really didn't want to be the new kid.

Often, when you're dreading something, it can feel as if there is just no possible way that whatever you're dreading will actually happen—as if some goddess of serendipity will surely swoop in and stop it in the nick of time. The test you haven't studied for will be rescheduled for next week; the guy you've really been meaning to break up with will tell you he's decided to move to India to embark upon a life of meditation but will always love you and remember the times you shared; the cockroaches in your apartment will be revealed to have been a very involved art project your roommate was working on, so you won't have to argue with the landlord and call the exterminator nine times and be afraid of going to the bathroom in the middle of the night for several weeks.

The goddess of serendipity almost never swoops in. I packed up my stuff and moved down the street.

It took me a few weeks to start feeling comfortable. In late May 2006, Reggie Love came down to the Hope Fund, too, and became my deputy. Reggie had graduated from Duke the year before, where he'd been a star on the football and basketball teams, and Possum hired him as an intern in the Senate office. By the time I understood how big my job really was, I knew I needed help, and Reggie was the guy. He started traveling with Obama on complicated political trips and helped me do outreach (checking in with supporters, tracking elections, etc.).

Obama was on the Senate Foreign Relations Committee, and he made his first trip to Africa that summer. Gibbs and Mark Lippert, our SFRC staffer, managed that trip, and Reggie and I focused on political travel and the plans for Obama's book tour for *The Audacity of Hope*, which would kick off in September.

While Obama was in Africa, I wrote the political plan for the 2006 midterms. A political plan is basically the who/what/when of the year: key people Obama should be seeing, major events that we should be planning around, and how it all fits together so that at the end of the year you can say, "We wanted to get XYZ done, and we did." (Or didn't.) It's also a very good way to make sure the most senior people and Obama are aligned on the mission. In Obama's case, we all felt like the midterm elections were his chance to really *arrive*—we saw how popular he was, he was getting all these crazy invitations, and we wanted him to use that momentum to be a workhorse on behalf of Democrats running for reelection. Our political plan included introducing him to labor leaders, state party activists across the country, and what we called "rising political stars"—people who were like him a few years earlier. (One of the people on that list was Eric Garcetti, now the mayor of LA; another was Cecilia Muñoz, who was at the Latino civil rights organization the National Council of La Raza at the time.) We wanted to make sure that, for all the fancy, high-profile people who would reach out to meet him, he was also spending time with lesser-known thought leaders. Obama himself felt this was important, too.

There are probably a lot of people in my job who would not have committed a plan like this to paper. It was ambitious and complicated. But I was raised in the Possum school of memo writing, and I think that he and Gibbs wanted to see what I would do. It was entitled "The Political Plan for the Best Candidate Not Running for President."

* * *

As soon as Obama came back from his trip to Africa, his publisher started calling. One after another, his book tour events were selling out. Would it be possible to move them to bigger venues?

On top of *The Audacity of Hope*, we layered on political and Hope Fund travel. Every candidate for House and Senate wanted Obama to headline their events. Senator Tom Harkin from Iowa invited him to the annual Steak Fry fund-raiser— THE place to be if you're a politician who wants to run for president or get national attention. Things were getting crazy.

Obama never faltered (and if he did, he was mostly joking). At one point, we were doing an event for Cory Booker in Newark, and from there we planned to fly Continental to Providence, where we had scheduled a fund-raiser for Sheldon Whitehouse, who was running for Senate. Halfway through Cory Booker's event, we got a note that all Continental flights had been canceled due to weather.

Bad! I got on the phone to try to find a private plane, a helicopter, anything that would get us up there; if senators managed to snag an event with Obama, they really looked forward to it. They raised so much more money, and the atmosphere was electric.

After a few calls, it seemed like there was nothing we could do. We couldn't get a private plane or a helicopter on such short notice. A train would take too long. But even though it would have been so much easier and we had every excuse to cancel, Obama was not going to let Sheldon Whitehouse down: "We don't disappoint our friends." He suggested we rent a car. I was not going to be in the driver's seat with Obama during bad-weather rush hour in Manhattan, but I was able to secure a car service, and Obama and I spent the trip up to Rhode Island reading *People* magazine in the back.

Some combination of me, Gibbs, Reggie, and the finance

directors for the Hope Fund, Jenny Yeager and Jordan Kaplan, crisscrossed the country with Obama for more than two months. Jenny and Jordan were fund-raisers and Obama originals from the Senate race; Jordan did the West, Jenny did the East, and today they are married with three kids. It was great. When you got back to the hotel every night you passed out cold, but the response to Obama was exhilarating.

We all spent a lot of time together. Jordan and I would get on Obama's nerves by singing in the car—Obama was always in the front with the volunteer driver, and like kids in the backseat on long trips, Jordan and I would sing along to whatever was on the radio. Once, when we were butchering a Motown song in the suburbs of Philadelphia, Obama snapped at us—he said something like, "Must you both?"—and we stopped immediately. We didn't know if we were in trouble; it felt like we were. But after a while the silence was deafening, and he told us we could sing again. Another time, after we had all been served Obama's traditionally healthy road meal of grilled salmon and brown rice, he noticed I wasn't touching my food. "Aren't you going to eat something?" he asked. I had gotten so sick of grilled salmon paired with a complex carbohydrate that I couldn't eat any more; I told him no, it was too boring. "Food is fuel," he replied, and went back to his dinner.

Obama also enjoyed gossiping about my dating life (or lack thereof). At an event at Lawrence Bender's house in Los Angeles, Gibbs and I were sitting in the den reading our BlackBerries when Obama came over and told me that he had "found someone" for me and that I should "get off the couch and come be social."

It turned out the person he'd "found" for me was Lawrence Bender himself—the man who produced *An Inconvenient Truth*, *Reservoir Dogs*, and almost all of Quentin Tarantino's movies afterward. I appreciated Obama's opinion of me, but I was pretty sure Lawrence Bender was not going to be interested in me, or even understand why Obama was dragging my ass up to talk to him. I stayed on the couch.

      ■   ■   ■

Things got a little more serious at the end of October, when around 5:00 one morning I got a call from Rahm Emmanuel, who was the chair of the Democratic Congressional Campaign Committee at the time—his job was to get more Democrats into the House and Senate. He told me John Kerry had said something batshit crazy while out campaigning hard for congressional candidates in the hopes of making another presidential run in 2008: He'd told a group of students in California that those unable to navigate the country's education system would "get stuck in Iraq."

This comment was really unfortunate, and Republicans pounced. They tried to make it sound like John Kerry thought our soldiers were dumb—that uneducated people end up in the military. That was absolutely not what he meant, but it didn't matter. Bush had won in 2004 by painting Kerry as aloof and unpatriotic. He was toast. Tim Walz—a candidate for the House from Minnesota—canceled Kerry's appearances in Mankato, and Rahm needed Obama and Hillary Clinton to cover all the events that Kerry was scheduled for that week.

Rahm and I brainstormed three or four stops Obama could

add to his next few days of travel. Talk about adrenaline; this was go time. We were singlehandedly going to take back the House and Senate! It felt like the country was finally turning against Bush and the Republicans, and some dumb gaffe wasn't going to slow our momentum. We wanted Obama to be leading the charge.

I talked to Gibbs and Possum, and we agreed on all the added stops. We would do a big roundup going into Election Day—Missouri, Iowa, and Tennessee again, and we would even hit Arkansas to campaign for Governor Mike Beebe. Not many Democrats, besides Bill Clinton, were requested in Arkansas. I went in and pitched the new schedule to Obama.

"Who do you work for?" he asked. "Me or Rahm?"

I did not take the bait. My job was to be confident in my recommendations. This was his moment, and we were taking it.

"Come on!" I replied. "WE HAVE TO WIN!"

He laughed, said of course, and we hit the road again.

We were doing election night in Chicago, and we had a little setup at the Hilton on Wacker where Obama would get incoming election results and be available for live interviews. During a few hours of downtime, I went to the Bloomingdale's on Michigan Avenue and bought a pair of very proper, very adult, very political director–y Isaac Mizrahi heels. I didn't need them—Obama wasn't formal—but I was starring in this very *West Wing* scene playing in my head, and in this scene I was not wearing Minnetonka moccasins.

The Democratic landslide started at around 7:00 PM. While Obama was doing interviews, we were calling so many candidates to congratulate them (and slyly take some credit for their margin of victory) that I didn't have enough cell phones to go around. We were happy. We had met some really terrific candidates on the road, people dedicated to public service who would undoubtedly have a positive impact in Washington, and it felt good. I didn't feel uncertain about my job anymore; I had risen to the occasion and taken the help I needed along the way.

Obama was still firm that he was not thinking about running for president in 2008, that he was just out there working hard for the class of 2006. But the rest of us were not so sure. I knew that if we were going to launch an exploratory committee, I would have to be ready.

*　*　*

There is no better time than when everyone wants you to do something but you haven't said yes yet. Many of the House and Senate candidates we'd worked with were saying Obama should run for president. Old political hands were saying they hadn't seen people respond to anyone like this since Bobby Kennedy. It's pretty hard to not let that shit go to your head, but you can't. There's a difference between being the flavor of the month and having staying power, and I really believe that Obama wasn't believing his own hype.

We campaigned for 32 candidates that election, and 31 won. (Sorry, Harold Ford.) I had even gotten a date out of the whole deal: When we were at the Steak Fry in Iowa, a terrible storm came through, and our flight was canceled, so Gibbs, Jordan, Obama, and I drove from Ames, Iowa, to Chicago in a rented PT Cruiser. We stopped at a Subway for dinner—Obama suggested it—and Obama started asking if I had noticed that one of Harkin's staffers seemed interested in me. I said no, I had not. We got in the car and kept driving. Finally, Obama turned to me and said, "Look, he was into you! You have to email him, and if you don't, I will." Unfortunately for me, in the Senate one's email address is very easy to figure out—first_last@XYZsenator'sname.senate.gov. So I emailed the guy and we went on a few dates.

A few days after Election Day, Obama was invited to give the keynote speech at the New Hampshire 100 Days dinner—the New Hampshire equivalent of the Harkin Steak Fry. If you ever want to run for president, you need to do this dinner.

The movement to get Obama to run was gaining some steam. Back at the Hope Fund—which was nicknamed the Hope Flood because it turned into an 800-square-foot swamp every time it rained; one of us had to be on call to come in and pick up all the boxes of *The Audacity of Hope* from the floor so they didn't get ruined—it felt like Santa's workshop heading into Christmas. Obama agreed to meet with a small group of us and talk about it. Possum even got Julianna Smoot—who had helped lead the Democratic Senatorial Campaign Committee to victory in 2006—to come in and discuss working on the campaign. It was always with the caveat of "If there were a campaign"—but still.

We met at Axelrod's office in Chicago a few times. He had advised Obama for many years, and at first the meetings consisted only of Gibbs, Smoot, Axe, Possum, and me. We picked up some people along the way—David Plouffe, Steve Hildebrand, Valerie Jarrett—and especially at the beginning, it was a lot of talk about how hard this would be. How hard running against Hillary Clinton—her machine, her money—would be. Obama was skeptical that we could mount an operation that would beat her.

Right before Christmas, Obama said he was going to Hawaii and would let us know what he had decided when he came back. Talk about pins and needles. I had said I wanted to work for Obama because I didn't want to work on a presidential campaign again, but I found myself really wanting to work on *his* presidential campaign. I hadn't been around for when John Kerry was deciding to run, so I didn't know his motivations, but having seen Obama's thought process, I was sure he would be doing it for the right reasons—to impact the country, to create real change. I thought that, even if we lost, we would be doing it for the right reasons.

Whenever my friends or family would ask me about whether Obama was really considering running, I would pretend not to know anything. I became a recluse and spent a lot of time in my apartment, going over every single thing I would need to set in motion if Obama came back from Hawaii and said, "Let's do it." I had notes posted all over my living room.

* * *

Hope Flood became the Obama Exploratory Committee headquarters on January 16, 2007, and it was one of the most exciting days of my life. Reprogramming the fax machine to say "Obama Exploratory Cmte" was exhilarating—I know it sounds ridiculous, but it really, really was. My weeks of reclusive brainstorming had paid off: I had a detailed time line of everything we needed to do. (Reprogramming the fax machine was on it.) Hope Flood wasn't posh to begin with, but it was transformed into a shelter for young fund-raising staffers, who sat around with their computers on their laps because we had no desks. I was still the political director for the Hope Fund, but that would soon change.

We all began to trawl craigslist looking for apartments in Chicago. The one bedrooms were really shitty and expensive, but the two bedrooms had potential. I saw Smoot on the phone with donors in the corner of the office; immediately, I eyed her like prey. An adult roommate would be my path to a sweet living situation.

When she walked by my desk, I turned around and said in my most casual voice, "Hey, Julianna . . . do you know where you're going to live in Chicago?"

"No," she replied. "I have no goddamn idea."

My opportunity to strike. I asked her if she wanted to be roommates.

"Fine," she said.

"I have a cat," I said.

"Fine," she replied, and walked away.

Smoot did not have time for pleasantries. She had just learned that our political email database had about 10,000 contacts in it. I thought that was a good thing; Reggie and I had been so slick in getting email addresses at all the events Obama attended that fall. But apparently it was anemic.

I started looking for short-term, furnished apartments—after all, I figured the chances that we would be out there for the entire two years before the election were pretty slim. We were very pumped, but becoming the Democratic nominee was a long shot.

At the same time as I was wrapping up life in DC, Cara, my best friend, was getting married. Her bridal shower and bachelorette weekend were right after we formed the OEC, and I was the maid of honor. On the train to BWI to go up to New York, I was on a conference call about the event where Obama would announce he was running for president. My phone cut out at the end, but I was almost at the airport, so I figured I would be able to get debriefed after I made it through security.

When I got to BWI and was standing in line for security, my phone rang. It was Larry Grisolano, one of Axe's partners. He told me what they had decided: Instead of one announcement event in Springfield and a second over the border in Iowa, which is what we had planned, they would do one event in Springfield, three in Iowa, one in New Hampshire, and one in Chicago. Over the course of three days.

At that point, I was the only person working in scheduling and advance for the exploratory committee. We didn't even have a credit card yet. It would fall on me to plan this.

I asked if he was trying to say they wanted a chartered plane for the whole trip, which would begin in about three weeks. Yes, that was what he was trying to say. They intended to transport press and some supporters, friends, and family, and this inevitably meant more staff would travel as well. I knew I was looking at managing the logistics of an additional 30 to 40 people more than I had planned. I would also have to find a plane big enough, on short notice, and make sure it could land in the airports near the cities they had picked and make sure those airports had stairs that fit the plane, which is not always the case.

I sat on the floor of BWI and started to sob uncontrollably. I couldn't believe how little concern they had for the amount of work this meant—not just work, but magic. TSA agents had to come sweep me away. They asked what was wrong; I told them I had to get a chartered plane with no credit card or stairs. They looked at me like I was insane and walked away.

I also needed a staff; where I would find one was less obvious. The scheduling and advance world was made up almost entirely of people who had cut their teeth with the Clintons in the '90s. The Hillary team had already started recruiting, and the message was clear: Do anything for Obama, and you are dead to us. I was screwed. My message was, "Dear God, please help me. I trust you enough to do Clinton events, too, please just help me, please, please, please."

It was the worst possible time to be heading up a raucous ladies' weekend. I landed in Albany and picked up the bachelorettes' white mega minivan—"the Vangina"—and I had coordinated the rest of the gang's train arrivals and pickups at the Poughkeepsie and Rhinecliff train stations. My mom was picking up all the booze, and my dad was making Cara's favorite pizza. The only thing I cared about was making this weekend great, and I knew the only way to make it great was to ask for some help and give orders.

There was no cell service in the house we rented, so each morning I got up at 5:00 AM and went to the house I grew up in—conveniently down the street—to check my email and phone messages. I answered everything and explained when I would be back on the grid. I kept a running list of what I needed to do and I got it done. As I type this, I feel like I should apologize to Cara for what was probably a rag-tag bachelorette weekend.

Still: We ate, we drank, we cruised around in the Van-gina. I think I kept it together and showed my hand only when I passed out early on Saturday night. As for the charter plane and Obama's announcement tour, I knew I had made it work at the end of the first full day. We were staying at an AmericInn in Iowa, and I was following Obama down the hallway when he turned around and said, "You're pretty proud of yourself, aren't you?"

CHAPTER 7

Humility, or Changes We Can Believe In, Sort Of, If We Have To

When Obama became president-elect in 2008, our team went through a big shift. The period between Election Day and Inauguration Day is appropriately referred to as "the transition," and there are two entities that support the president-elect during this time: the Presidential Transition Team (PTT) and the Presidential Inaugural Committee (PIC).

We were all friends, Obama included, and although we were working for him, he always maintained a casual atmosphere—even in moments of crisis. Once, he asked me if I was angry with him because, in the Senate, I would refer to him as "Senator Obama" instead of "Barack." He was not one who engaged in or enjoyed formality; later, when he was the president and I was deputy chief, Nancy-Ann DeParle and I would often ride in a different car when we all went to meetings and events—so we could get work done and give him some privacy—and he eventually got upset and asked her if she didn't like sitting with him. (She told him she assumed he'd like some time to himself.) But when I started working for him in early 2005, he was the junior senator from Illinois and the youngest member of the Senate. If people like me and Favs and Tommy ran around calling him "Barack" in front of people like Ted Kennedy and Robert C. Byrd, what reason would they have to respect him? (We ultimately brokered a deal that, in front of other senators, I would call him Senator Obama, but otherwise it was Barack.)

During the transition, I worked for the PTT, but I also had a hand in the PIC. This wasn't my ideal situation; the PIC would have been the cherry on top of the 2008 campaign for me. Preparing the inaugural events for the first African American president—there was nothing more important, or exciting, in my opinion. But Obama had asked me to stay in Chicago with him on the PTT while I kept an eye on the PIC. I knew that staying in Chicago was the most important thing I could do for my boss (this wasn't *my* inauguration) and that my deputy on the campaign, Emmett, would be an excellent executive director of the PIC, so I let it go. Pretty easily.

Generally, though, this was a very anxious time. First, neither group offers a permanent job. You try to do your best on your current assignment—whether that's PIC or PTT— but you can't help but worry you're somehow missing out on locking down a gig in the administration because you're distracted by the president-elect's immediate needs. You kind of have to have faith.

Second, at the very end of the campaign, department

heads—of which I was one—are given a grid on which they have to grade their staff. Unlike at Ivy League colleges—cough, cough—you can give only a certain number of As and Bs. I didn't exactly know how the grade I gave people would be used, or know how much influence it would have on how my people would be placed—especially since I didn't agree with having to give people Cs!—so I felt weird about this, too. Rumor had it that in previous administrations, scheduling and advance staff had gotten lost in the shuffle and didn't end up with great jobs in the White House. So not only was I worried about myself, but I needed to make sure that my team was on the big radar.

On top of all that, going to the DC PTT office felt like you were visiting a prison: You walked in and handed your ID through a plastic barrier, and then you waited in uncomfortable plastic chairs under harsh lighting for someone to come "escort you in." You had to go through magnetometers. One day I walked in and saw Plouffe looking like he was waiting to be arraigned. The PIC was not better; it was in an old DC building that was hard to get to and had very little heat, and this was winter. Standard attire there was a hoodie over a suit.

I spent most of November and December in the Chicago PTT office, which was where Obama was a lot of the time; it was a little better than the DC office. It was here that we would meet to discuss the short lists for positions in the Cabinet and who should come out to meet with Obama. We also brainstormed who would be great for which jobs, made lists for inaugural invites, and got a taste of what life in the government would be like.

As a taxpayer, you're probably stoked to hear that there is no "entertainment" budget for the PTT. That government employees have no way to expense food or drink or be reimbursed for boxes of tissues that they bought for the office when everyone had the flu. For PTT employees, it meant that we didn't have glasses or pitchers to serve water; this may seem like the least of your necessities, but we had meetings and conferences with a lot of people there. Once, Ferial had to walk to Bed Bath & Beyond in a snowstorm to buy pitchers, utensils, water, and apple juice for a meeting we were having with then Senator Clinton. We still don't know where the idea for apple juice came from—Senator Clinton was definitely not in kindergarten at the time—but it doesn't matter: Ferial lugged it all back to the office. Each night after that, she and I took the pitchers and forks home to wash because the only sinks we had were in the bathroom, and they were too shallow and didn't have hot water.

All the support we'd had on the campaign—or even in the Senate—was stripped away. We weren't exactly feeling like hot shit because we were about to go work in the White House. When Obama was having an economic meeting and heard it was Peter Orszag's birthday—Peter was going to be the director of the Office of Management and Budget—he wanted to get a cake, and all we could think was, *ARRRGHHHHH, plates?!?!?!?*

I also worked with Mel Winter, Michelle Obama's deputy chief of staff, on coordinating some of the inauguration. Mel and I had to learn how to do Excel spreadsheets in order to make the friends-and-family guest list. (Don't laugh—

you can't do them either, and this was in 2008.) She would read the names aloud from handwritten notes POTUS and FLOTUS had made, and I would type them in. We did this a lot. One day, we were going through POTUS's family, who were traveling from outside the United States, and Mel read aloud to me, "Abongo Obama." I said, "Is that with an *O* or an *A*?" Because the office was so small, Obama heard us and shouted back, "Are you making fun of my family?"

He was just messing with us. Still, when Obama walked by, we no longer said "Hey" and kept working—we stood up. He would tell us to sit back down, but we always stood up.

* * *

In late November, I was offered the job of assistant to the president and director of scheduling and advance, and I made the move from Chicago to DC in early December.

It was strange to be back in DC. I had really loved living in Chicago, and were it not for us winning, I probably would have stayed. My apartment was in a new building in a sort of charmless part of town—13th and M Streets NW—but it was walking distance from the White House, so I signed the lease without seeing it. I bought my furniture from Crate and Barrel after two glasses of champagne, and after my years of moving around it was the first real furniture I had ever owned.

As I pulled up to the PTT office on my first full day in DC, I saw Joe Paulsen standing on the corner, appearing to be hailing a cab. Joe had started on the campaign in Iowa. When the caucus was over, I was so impressed that I asked him to come work for me in Chicago. I had him handle highly complicated and sensitive situations, like the logistics around the Commission on Presidential Debates. When I got out of the car, we hugged, and I asked what he was doing. He was totally frazzled; he really was hailing a cab. But not for himself—for his new boss, who was on the national security team and whom I had never heard of. I was kind of shocked. *Uh, David Plouffe hailed his own cabs*, I thought. *Who is the self-important nobody making Joe do this?*

That was the DC transition in a nutshell: I saw people I had found incredibly capable hailing cabs and making copies. My heart kind of sank. Was this how it was going to be?

Sort of. Some of the "cavalry"—people who had served in previous administrations, who didn't really respect us newbies all that much—seemed to enjoy being back in the saddle. Many of the people on the PTT team in DC were former Clinton staffers who were glad to be offered more work but didn't have such warm feelings for Team Obama. One of the main things I remember is that they used acronyms we couldn't decipher; *BLUF* (Bottom Line Up Front) is the main one. People would come at you like, "Give me the BLUF," and we would all look at one another and mouth the words, "Do you know what that is?" I had a constant stomachache in this office.

For two years, Plouffe had led a group that was structured but very open, and because of that—because he treated everyone equally—no one ever really fussed or jockeyed for power. We had run a campaign on believing change was actually possible. But Plouffe had almost nothing to do

with the transition, so once we got to DC—which is hier-
archical and patriarchal—it felt like the same old backslappy
white-bro club. These old-school government hacks considered your career impressive if you had worked for several
administrations, not if you had been on a campaign that
had accomplished something many people had believed was
impossible. This didn't work in my favor. I was treated like I
didn't know what the hell I was doing, even though none of
these guys had worked for a president in a post–9/11 world,
when the kinds of events the Secret Service will permit you
to do are fundamentally different from what they were before
the attacks. My job required more creativity and planning to
build great, impactful events—especially because the Secret
Service was even less willing to do anything remotely risky
with the first black president.

My team had built a great relationship with the Secret
Service during the two years we were on the campaign, and I
knew we had a long time left together. So when someone on a
conference call suggested that we have Obama do an event on
the George Washington Bridge—yes, standing in the middle
of the bridge—I didn't hesitate to say it wouldn't work. Even
though I was right, I could hear people rolling their eyes over
the phone; some of them actually continued talking over me.
I will never know if it was because I was a 32-year-old woman
or because I was a 32-year-old person or because I just didn't
have "White House" on my résumé, but my opinions were
always discounted, when they were even solicited at all.

I spent some time feeling very defensive and uneasy. Information was the tool I needed to do my job, and I couldn't

figure out where it was or how to get it. One day, Dey and I were talking about mapping out the first 100 days. Rahm Emanuel—who was going to be chief of staff in the White House—overheard us and said, "Mona has the block calendar." This was shocking. We had always been the keepers of the block calendar—it was like the scheduler's bible, and not just anyone could have access to it. We also had no idea who Mona was.

We later learned that Mona was about to be announced as the White House deputy chief of staff for policy. Which was well and good, but why did she have our block? Why did Rahm have her start doing the schedule? By the time Mona left the White House two years later, we were buds and I lovingly called her Mo-Mo, but I never found out. Were it not for the team we had built—and the sense of community within our department that endured even though we were split between cities and offices—I think a lot of people would have bailed.

■ ■ ■

As Inauguration Day grew closer, once a week or so, Mel and I would head over to the Hay–Adams Hotel, where the first family was staying with Emmett, to talk about plans for the inauguration. Those meetings were some of the few times things felt familiar. We would talk about who needed to sit where, the status of certain events, and things like who the Obamas wanted to sing the national anthem and read as the poet laureate. Soon, I realized that I would be too busy preparing for the first day in the White House to see any of it.

As we headed into the holidays, things got into more of a flow, but I was fried. I went home to Rhinebeck for Christmas and acted like a real asshole—it was like I was getting my period for the first time. I was short-tempered, and my annoying, nitpicky attitude drove my whole family nuts. I started crying in the middle of Christmas Eve dinner. I was feeling so suffocated and overwhelmed by what was coming, but everyone was so proud of me. I should have been ecstatic, but I was mostly just scared. I didn't know how to talk about it without sounding ungrateful, so I just lashed out.

Dealing with the inauguration is a little bit like being a bouncer at an exclusive club in New York: Lots of people want in, but only certain people have tickets, and only certain other people have really, really good tickets. We had to make lists, prioritize, and try to make everyone as happy as possible. I found myself meeting people on street corners in Georgetown to exchange envelopes of very valuable goods. Even though I knew I couldn't go, my family—Mom, Pop, Moose, and Volpes (Cara couldn't make it because she was in labor)—got prime seats ("seats" being the key word) right in front of the Capitol.

The official festivities kicked off three days before the Tuesday inauguration, and the hottest ticket was the Lincoln Memorial concert on Sunday. Bono would be performing our campaign theme song, "City of Blinding Lights," which we had picked sitting around a conference room table in Springfield, Illinois, because we loved the intro; great entrance music should give you goose bumps. Beyoncé, Bruce Springsteen, Mary J. Blige, Denzel Washington, Pete Seeger, and

Laura Linney would also be performing. Dey and I were at the transition office in DC taking turns jumping up and down so the motion-sensor lights would kick back on.

On Monday night, inauguration eve, Dey and Jess slept over at my apartment because road closures would make it impossible for people to get to work. On Inauguration Day, Dey and I would be sworn in, and then we had to start preparing the schedule and setting up events for the president's first full day in office.

I met Dey and Jess at my apartment, and my downstairs neighbor, Anne, who was a friend from Chicago, came to join us. We all went to bed early, and in the morning we had Eggo waffles and mimosas and watched the inauguration coverage as we were getting ready—a very surreal sleepover. After Jess went off to man her inauguration post, Dey and I put on our suits, sneakers, and about eight layers to walk to the White House; it was fucking cold and a little slick. We took our dresses for the inaugural ball with us because we thought it would be too dicey to try to get home and come back.

Entering the Indian Treaty Room in the Eisenhower Executive Office Building (EEOB), we immediately found ourselves among a ton of people we didn't know, a lot of them acting like hot shit. People were scheduled to come in waves throughout the day; we filled out our employment forms with about 30 other new staff. When we stood up, raised our right hands, and were sworn in, it was a pretty standard procedure, but it should have been a real moment. If we hadn't been so anxious, we might have enjoyed it a bit more.

We parted ways after that. I headed over to the West

Wing, and Dey, who was deputy assistant to the president and director of scheduling, went to our offices in the EEOB.

I don't think Dey and I ever changed out of our sneakers that day. A *New York Times* article described the feeling of the president's first full day in office as being like "the first day of school"; for us, it was sort of like that, if not making it to sixth period on time would cause the United States government to screech to a halt. Obama had to do actual things—like have meetings in the Situation Room—that no one around him knew how to facilitate yet. We found out there were protocols for using certain rooms (i.e., the Cabinet Room is only for meetings with the Cabinet or congressional leadership), and figuring them out took so long. Some rooms you couldn't use for live press events because the copper wiring blocked signals. How do you book a meeting in the Situation Room? What kind of security clearance did people need to have? We didn't even have computer log-ins. When someone came in to teach us all how to use Timepiece, the software that allows you to make the White House schedule, I almost cried. It was impossible, and we had to use it that day.

We'd had the campaign down to an actual science. We had managed our department's $68 million general election budget within dollars and were able to go to Plouffe that fall and tell him he could take money back because we were on track to come in under budget by $3 million through the end of the campaign. (Anytime you can tell your boss or someone higher up that you have saved them money, do it.) We planned about three events a day, seven days a week, and that was just for POTUS. By the time we hit full speed after the convention in Denver, we were managing Barack, Michelle, Biden, Dr. B, and a slew of other high-profile surrogates like Ted and Caroline Kennedy, Jay Z, Bruce Springsteen, and Oprah. Except for the time we accidentally played Kanye West's "Touch the Sky" at an event for senior citizens a few weeks before the Iowa Jefferson–Jackson Day dinner, we ran like a well-oiled machine.

But this? This was hard. There were so many rules and protocols for the White House: Noncommissioned officers' names cannot appear on memos to the president; cabins on AF1 are ordered by seniority, and you can walk back on the plane but are not supposed to walk forward into a more senior cabin; in the Cabinet Room, the president always sits with his back to the Rose Garden in the chair in the middle with a slightly higher back, the vice president sits across from him, and the Cabinet secretaries representing the oldest departments—like State and Defense—have to go closest to the president. Just when you thought you had them all in order, someone came to you with more rules. The dress I was supposed to wear to the inaugural ball stayed in its bag in my office for two years. I never put it on and actually forgot it was there.

I am making this sound Very Bad partially because I did not expect it to be so bad. This is what the president's first public schedule looked like:

1:15PM: President Obama addresses staff and Cabinet secretaries (pool press)

2:30PM: President Obama attends White House open
house (pool press, base of staircase, on the ground level
by State Room)

3:15PM: President Obama meets with economic advisers
in the Roosevelt Room (closed press)

4:15PM: President Obama meets with Iraq military
advisers (closed press)

That's it. This is the schedule that kept me from getting
to the inaugural ball the night before. This.

It wasn't all chaos; we learned some fun things, too. For
example: The current Cabinet Room table was purchased in
1970 by President Nixon using personal funds. On her very
last day in the White House on January 19, 1977, Betty Ford
passed by the empty Cabinet Room and decided to take off
her shoes and dance on it because she had always wanted to.

People were telling us stuff like this as we were trying to
find the appropriate room for the president to address senior
staff and Cabinet members on his first day. We didn't want
to send out the schedule with the wrong room, and it was so
hard to get all the protocols straight that it took a very long
time.

When we finally thought we had figured it out—and
when we got our computers up and running—we sent an
email to the senior staff to lay out our plan. One member of
the team, who we were pretty certain was writing to us from
a cush seat in the presidential viewing stands at the inaugural parade, responded, "This is the most half-baked thing I
have ever seen." And we didn't even know why.

We finally figured out Room 450 was an acceptable solution and called it a day at around 8:00 PM. Dey left in the nick of time to meet her boyfriend and slog through one of the inaugural balls. I walked home—not because I wanted exercise but because the roads were still all closed; it was freezing, and the streets looked like a scene from a Cold War movie. I ate a Lean Cuisine, slammed a glass of wine, and wondered what the hell could be in store for tomorrow.

There are moments when you catch yourself wondering how you look walking off Marine One—wind blowing in your hair, serious leather bag at your side, adjacent to the man who runs the country. There are also times when you actually walk off Marine One with the president on a Friday afternoon in rural Virginia, climb into your armored Suburban, and are told by a member of the medical team that you have split your skirt clear up to the zipper. Those are the moments you should remember: when your coworkers are rallying around you to keep you from showing the president your really old Hanes Her Way underwear. When they pin you together and you have to lie sort of sideways in a mermaid position so you don't bust the pins.

This is not an elaborate scenario I made up to illustrate the importance of humility—it really happened. I attribute a lot of my success to never losing sight of the fact that I worked for Barack Obama. I was not Barack Obama; I am never going to be Barack Obama. In DC, you can get some level of power from the person you work for, but the minute you forget power comes and goes with elections, that's it. You may think you are hot shit for working at the White

House, but there is always hotter shit around the corner. You are staff, a helpfully lowly term.

* * *

Around six months before David and I got engaged, I went to a dinner being held in honor of UK prime minister David Cameron's visit to America. It was a big deal; everyone in the White House was excited about it. I would be wearing vintage. David never really cared about stuff like this, so I brought Dey as my plus-one.

The day of the event, David had lunch with Jeff Shell, the chairman of NBC Universal International at the time, and during the dinner, David texted me to say Jeff was there and that I should say hi. I had been to a lot of black-tie events by this point, but the gravity of the company was always a little intimidating, even while I was wearing a fabulous dress and had knocked back a champagne. Jeff was at a table with Anna Wintour and her partner. I tapped Jeff on the shoulder, introduced myself, and said I'd heard he'd had lunch with David that day. Jeff recognized me immediately. "Oh," he responded warmly, "David's the best. You guys are going to be just like Susan Sarandon and Tim Robbins, living together forever but never getting married!"

Everyone froze. "Oh *dear*," Anna said, looking up and lowering her head in that skeptical way she does. I had been able to pass off other people's "You're an old lady who will never get married!" faux pas before, but this was humiliating.

I went back to David's house at around midnight—we weren't technically living together, because I went back to my apartment every morning to change clothes before work, but my cat lived at David's—and I was livid.

"Do you know what just happened to me?" I yelled at the sleeping man.

"What?" he asked, very groggy.

"You told Jeff Shell that we were going to be like Susan Sarandon and Tim Robbins?" I went downstairs and watched TV.

Even after he changed his mind and proposed to me in front of the Georgetown Domino's, I had a very difficult time accepting that he had come around. Shrummie and I officially moved into David's place after we got engaged, and I was a wreck. I wish that I had tried to live with a boyfriend sooner than age 37, even if I knew we would probably, eventually break up, because I was deeply, almost bizarrely uneasy about moving in with David. I felt like a burden, or an intruder, or like I'd tricked him into proposing to me. I kept my apartment, still paying rent, for about eight months after I moved in with him. I also kept all my Crate and Barrel furniture there, just in case; David had much nicer stuff, but I never felt like it was mine, and I didn't feel like I could bring any of my things to the house because all my things were from Crate and Barrel. I cried a lot.

When we got married, it was even harder, because it was legal. I couldn't get over the money thing, and instead of a little nagging sense that I was barging in and toppling over David's high-flying bachelor lifestyle, the marriage made our relationship feel officially imbalanced. What could I possibly be adding to our life? I was constantly doing calculations in my head, thinking about how much the impressiveness of my job at the White House, or my skill at making granola, or my cat, was potentially "worth" to my husband— like I was trying to tally up a bizarro-feminist dowry. I had a savings account without much in it, and for probably eight years, I had done all my finances in a Barbra Streisand notebook; when it ran out of pages, I just added more. David had an accountant and stock. I guess I would often talk about what I was "bringing to the table," because one day he told me, "Stop using the word *contribute*—we are married."

The actual planning and implementation of the wedding also gave me anxiety, and we didn't even have a wedding. We were going to, but it just seemed like too much work, especially for two people with very busy jobs. When older people get married, the guest lists are already long, but one night we went to Meiwah and decided to try to sketch out a list of people we would have to invite. It looked like something out of *Us Weekly*. David's list in particular looked like a Kardashian who got into politics: Senate majority leader, Senate minority leader, all the way down to staff assistants. He wrote for so long after I was done that I think I ordered another wine. My family would have gotten there and been like, "Who are you? This is ridiculous." It was my job to plan very elaborate and stressful events, and I didn't want anyone to have to go through that for me. We decided to skip a big wedding.

Unfortunately—or fortunately, if you espouse a mergers-and-acquisitions perspective on wardrobes—we did not make this decision before I bought a wedding dress. A few weeks before the Meiwah Accords, I had gone on a short trip to Chicago, and when I met up with Anne, Julianna, and Stephanie Cutter (a friend who had a series of roles in the Obama family), for what I thought would be an afternoon of expensive salads and cocktails, they surprised me with appointments to look at wedding dresses.

It was so, so nice of them, and I was completely mortified. As we walked up the steps to the first shop, I turned to the group and said, "OK, guys, I'm going to do this, but I really don't want it to be a scene."

We opened the doors and Austin Scarlett, from the first season of *Project Runway*, was having a trunk show.

When you watch an episode of *Say Yes to the Dress*, you don't see all the scaffolding necessary to maneuver a normal-size woman into a sample-size wedding gown. All of a sudden, the tasteful, elegant person you think you are goes out the window; I was surprised and disappointed to learn that bungee cords would be required to get me into the dresses I wanted to try on. Maybe it says something about how susceptible I am to patriarchal narratives about the lasting importance of a woman's wedding day, but instead of thinking the whole thing was ridiculous, at one point I found myself in a jewel-encrusted peplum dress with a "vanity sheet" covering my butt, and I earnestly turned to my friends and asked, "How do I look?"

Awful. I tried on some Jenny Packhams, which made me feel like Princess Kate, and then we went to Vera Wang. Vera gave us champagne, which helped, but the dresses were heavy and unflattering. I didn't want to go anywhere else, so I suggested we give up—though it was a fun, nice gesture—and go to Freds, the restaurant at Barneys.

Everyone thought this was a great idea, but I wonder if it was because they knew they could get me drunk. After a couple of cocktails, they were all saying, "Come on, one more place! It's just around the corner!" I went on the condition that it would be a purely academic excursion and everyone would only pick dresses that it would be "fun" to try on.

This was a much better experience. But when we were about to leave—this always happens—Julianna came back with a beaded, one-of-a-kind Valentino runway and said, "Alyssa, I know this looks crazy, but you should try it on."

It was $13,000 and I bought it on a payment plan.

I want to pause here to say that buying a $13,000 designer wedding dress was not something I ever thought I would do. When I was growing up, I never dreamed of the perfect wedding or cared much about having the nicest, most expensive things. I also could not really afford it; I had tried very hard to save money while I worked in government, so this was not going to destroy me, but it was still a stupid purchase. Beautiful, but dumb. David later offered to pay for it, but I wouldn't tell him how much it cost, and I didn't want him to anyway.

Still, it looked good. We went to the restaurant in Ralph Lauren and had steak Diane to celebrate that I'd bought a dress that costs the same amount as a Nissan Versa.

■ ■ ■

After we decided to ditch the real wedding, there was still the problem of the venue: Would we just go to City Hall? Would we have even a little party?

I thought we should. But it was not the best time: health care.gov was still failing, and the government shutdown, which happened about a month and a half before I got married, was sapping all my energy. I oversaw preparations for the shutdown as well as for the reopening, and in the middle we had to follow yet more protocols. I came to work because, as an assistant to the president, I was permitted to; most other people couldn't use their BlackBerries, access their emails, or come into the office. This included the cleaning staff. White House operators recorded a script for answering the phones, something like: "Thank you for calling the White House. Due to the government shutdown, we can't help you." It was sort of nice in some ways; you had senior people answering their own phones and doing dirty work, which created this sense of camaraderie. No one acted like a diva. If someone (approved) was coming in for a meeting, I cleaned the bathroom stalls, made sure the garbage cans weren't overflowing, and refilled the toilet paper.

When it became obvious that planning even the most basic wedding would be too much, someone told me that Elena Kagan and Sonia Sotomayor loved officiating at the Supreme Court. This seemed great. I bought a short Stella McCartney dress from Farfetch (blue with wide sleeves), and we scheduled a Friday afternoon with Justice Kagan, who was glad to have us.

On the day of my wedding, I acted like a savage animal. When people have big weddings, to defuse their nerves, they fixate on the flowers not being right or a bridesmaid being late; when it's just the two of you, you have to confront your fear and destiny head on, and because I didn't know how to say I was nervous, I was really mean.

This was totally disproportionate to the kindness everyone showed me. After waking up scared, I went to get my hair done—the first mistake of the day. I should have just gotten a blowout, but the women at the salon told me I should get something different because it was my wedding day. Shortly after, I cried. My friend Stephanie showed up at the salon with champagne and hummus because "you have to see someone on your wedding day." Even though I wasn't there, my team decorated my office with a banner that read "Goodbye Single Alyssa" and did a photo shoot with it to show me over text messages. I pay it forward by advising all my friends who get married that, because it is so nerve-racking, they should just drink all day or take a Xanax.

When we got to the court, DK was looking cool, calm, and completely the opposite of me, so I freaked out more. As we were getting ready, he came over to me, smiling and nice and the way you would want a man to be on the day he is marrying you, and said, "I got you a gift." I was so stressed that I hissed back, "I didn't fucking get you anything!" *How dare he get me a gift?* For some reason, he gave it to me anyway; it was a pair of diamond earrings. I felt awful.

Justice Kagan had decorated her office with a "Happy Wedding!" sign, gotten a bottle of champagne, and put out an orchid (a symbol of love). She asked us what vows we wanted to use.

I was not prepared for this. "What are the options?" I replied. She showed them to us, and I was so overwhelmed that I just said, "What's the shortest one?" David was completely horrified and possibly questioning his choice to spend the rest of his life with me. I started drinking the champagne as soon as we had said our vows.

From the Supreme Court, we went back to the house, got our bags, took a picture with Shrummie, and went to stay at the Capella Hotel in Georgetown. We had dinner at 6:15, and I fell asleep by 9:00.

There's not a real resolution here, except the lesson that you should be able to accept the fact that sometimes you'll fuck up, have to sincerely apologize, and try to move on. The next morning, I woke up and watched the Ina Garten Thanksgiving special and felt normal again, except for being extremely embarrassed. We went back to our house—our honeymoon in New Zealand was booked for a few weeks later—and I said I was sorry for acting so ungrateful and unhappy; I didn't feel ungrateful or unhappy. I keep trying to find a place to wear the Valentino, but I feel like it should be in front of David, so it remains in my closet unworn.

CHAPTER 8

Risk-taking, or Ah-LEES-ah Goes to Brooklyn

We take a lot of different kinds of risks in the course of a day or a lifetime, but I tend to divide them into everyday, experiential, reputational, and personal/financial. Here are some examples:

EVERYDAY:
- Crossing the street against the light
- Stopping for coffee even though you know it might make you late for a meeting
- Getting a new haircut or trying a new salon
- Bringing up a new idea in a meeting without having bounced it off anyone

EXPERIENTIAL:
- Eating street meat in Bombay even though you suffer from IBS
- Going to Japan to visit your friend David Fogel and traveling the entire coast on a motorcycle for two

weeks (we got pulled over only once; you can't ride two-to-a-bike in Tokyo, but everywhere else it's fine!)
- Singing karaoke
- Going to a birthday party at a multifloor dance club and letting a man who says he's a Welsh paratrooper walk you home

REPUTATIONAL:
- Agreeing to write a book
- Defending a friend who is being attacked on Twitter when you know only half the story
- Praising an article you didn't read all the way through
- Working for a candidate or campaign

PERSONAL/FINANCIAL:
- Breaking up with a boyfriend or girlfriend
- Quitting your job, or not accepting a "good job" that isn't right
- Moving to a new city
- Going back to school

I was getting ready to leave the White House right around the time I got married, at the end of 2013. I felt like I had no choice—I was exhausted; I was irritable; I couldn't sleep without Tylenol PM or Ambien; I hadn't had a good idea in months. But I was still very nervous. I talked about it to only a handful of people outside before I actually announced I was going to do it.

As I was preparing to resign, friends were other-level generous in setting up introductory meetings for me with people in various industries around the country. They had to be discreet, since it still wasn't public that I was leaving, but they were still so helpful.

I knew Anna Wintour from working with her on Obama's 2008 and 2012 campaigns, and she was one of the supporters I was lucky enough to build a relationship with. She developed our Runway to Change and Runway to Win programs, which had designers producing Obama merchandise. (We sold out of them in record time; I still wear my Tracy Reese sweatshirt.) She gives advice the way you want it— straight. When we met for tea the winter before I announced I would leave the White House, she told me it was "time to go on to something new" and said if anything came to mind, she would let me know. Then she finished her tea, put her sunglasses on, and went to her next meeting. She calls me "Ah-LEES-ah."

About a month later, after I had announced my resignation and was preparing to leave later in the year, I got an email from her saying she'd sat next to Bill de Blasio—who had just been elected mayor of New York City a couple of months earlier—at a dinner and given him my number. How killer—she really was thinking of things I might be good at.

As I was reading her email (at a stop sign with no one behind me—don't text and drive), the phone rang through the Bluetooth on my car. It was a 917 number.

Bill de Blasio on the blower!

He introduced himself and said he thought I might be a good candidate to be commissioner of New York City's

Office of Emergency Management (OEM). Would I come speak with him?

The OEM, or, now, NYC Emergency Management, and its team—responders, planners, watch commanders, logisticians, community outreach, communications, and other staff—is responsible for planning and preparing for emergencies, educating the public about preparedness, coordinating emergency response and recovery, and collecting and disseminating emergency information. I had learned so much about emergency management while working at the White House, and it was one of the things I had enjoyed most—it was a way to have a real and immediate impact. But OEM had historically been run by a military chief or a captain (men). There was a part of me that worried, rightly or wrongly, that taking the helm of OEM might be the makings of the next installment of *Legally Blonde*. But that had also always been my thing: small but mighty, cheerfully girlfriend-y but hardworking, only an asshole when vitally necessary. I was imagining myself wearing a puffy vest and wellies on the cover of *New York* magazine already.

I set up a time to go see him the following week, and when I got there, I found City Hall pretty exciting—people getting the people's work done. It's also quite beautiful. De Blasio is famous for running late, and this day was no different, but Jess had left the White House and was the deputy chief of staff for the mayor at the time, so I chatted with her for a bit as I waited.

By the time he was ready to meet with me, he was very rushed. Or at least I felt like he was rushed. One thing about Obama: He deeply believes in running on time, and we worked very hard to set up his days so that he would. He never wanted people who traveled to come see him to be kept waiting.

I was a decidedly outside-the-box choice for this job. I had earned the respect of the Secret Service and members of the WH Military Office, but while this, too, was an agency that had been always been led by men in uniform, I wasn't assured the same result here. In the White House, I built the relationships that made me successful for two years before I took the helm.

I had a list of questions for the mayor; the most important was "How would you set me up for success?" Generally, if you're coming in to take over a department, you want to know that your boss will demonstrate to everyone else that you have his or her support. You also want to know whether you get to hire people or make staffing or structural changes.

De Blasio's answer did not make me feel better; it was something to the effect of "They [the OEM staff] would need to get with what's happening." Still, I put that aside; this was a big and important job that I felt would take my career to the next level. If I was successful, I could really make a difference. If not, everyone in New York would blame me for a future hurricane. And they might not be wrong to do so.

As we were winding down the conversation—him checking his BlackBerry throughout—he cut to the chase pretty quickly and asked if I would want this job, and he added that he'd need me to start no later than May 1. This was an aggressive way to close, since I had said I was interested but that was about it; I was by no means in love with the idea. I explained there was no way I could leave the president and be installed in New York by May 1. I had promised POTUS I wouldn't leave until May, and I also needed a fucking break.

De Blasio said something like, "POTUS had you long enough, and he needs to let you go. It will be fine."

I was speechless. My eyes darted around his office looking for something to focus on. I was biting the inside of my cheek to avoid saying something rude. Was he talking about *my* POTUS? There was no way I was going to (1) leave POTUS earlier than I said I would; (2) work for a person who wanted me to let down my old boss—a man who, in addition to having given me every opportunity in the world, was *the president of the United States*; and (3) not take a break between jobs.

I made Jess walk me out and told her that the conversation had given me a stomachache. It was sunny but cold. I was starving because I hadn't eaten breakfast before the meeting, and I had waited so long for the mayor that I was now overdue for lunch. The streets were slushy, but I walked for a bit before sitting down. I was very concerned about what I would do—and who I would be—when I left the White House, and this had seemed like such a perfect, meant-to-be opportunity. It was really disappointing.

Even if I could have managed without a break (that would have been crazy) or asked POTUS to let me leave as soon as possible (he would have said it was OK, but that's not how I wanted to go), I couldn't take a job where people's lives were in my hands and I didn't feel confident that I had what I needed to be successful. It was a risk I didn't want to take. I had worked hard to build a reputation, and I wasn't going to throw that away—I knew there would be another opportunity. I hadn't always believed that, but the older you get, the more confident you can be about what you're good at. The more places you can see where you belong.

*   *   *

On that same 36-hour trip to New York, my friend Maneesh was hosting an event for one of his companies, and he invited me to be interviewed by Charlie Rose. It would be off the record but in front of a live audience of about 200 entrepreneurs.

I agreed, obviously—I mean, it was Charlie Rose—but I was wary. I hadn't done an interview in years, and Charlie is such an icon; I was probably more worried about looking like a ditz in front of him specifically than I was about fucking it up in general. I killed a glass of sauvignon blanc to chill me out, and the show was under way.

It was a great interview. After the first five minutes, it felt like I was talking to an old friend onstage. (This is, I suspect, because Charlie Rose has been interviewing people for decades and is extremely good at it.) At the end of the event, Charlie invited me to be on his show. I was very flattered, but I assumed he was being polite. His office followed up the next day to lock in a date for me to appear as a guest for the entire hour on *The Charlie Rose Show*.

This was more than my brain could handle. My last television interview was after the Obama Exploratory Committee launched in early 2007, and our deputy press secretary, Bill Burton, convinced me to do a spot with Chris Wallace for *Fox News Sunday*. He said it would be "easy," "fluff," "light"— 10–15 minutes max. I asked what kind of prep I needed, and he said I "would be fine."

Luckily, I did not take Bill's word for it. I called my friend Stephanie Cutter and told her that I had agreed to do *Fox News Sunday*. Cutts is a media consultant and excellent herself at TV. She understood the gravity of the situation and gave me a crash course on how to answer questions I didn't know the answer to. Cutts is kind of like Liam Neeson in *Taken*; she doesn't sugarcoat. She didn't tell me that I would be fine. She said, "This is going to be hard and here is what you need to do to survive." (To survive, any time you get tripped up, just say, basically: "I agree with Barack Obama's stated position." Works in all situations, not just on TV.)

My Fox segment went on for more than 60 minutes and included questions on Iraq and Afghanistan. By the middle of the interview, I had sweat all the way through my Rebecca Taylor T-shirt and thought for sure I had pit stains on my jacket. At least it wasn't live. They edited the 60 minutes down to seven, and it wasn't horrible, but it definitely wasn't good. Did I really want to do that again?

* * *

When I did the risk-reward math, this was worth it: It was Charlie Rose. I set the date and became increasingly edgy every day that passed as it got closer. I thought about viable excuses to cancel. Every time I casually mentioned that I would be taping the show, someone would ask how I was getting ready for it, which was annoying, because I had really meant it as more of a "Honey, does this dress make me look fat?" kind of comment.

A few days before the interview, some of the comms team came by my office for a prep session. They drilled me on POTUS positions, gave me stats on how many people had signed up via healthcare.gov, and told me how to frame information on recent polls (which weren't great for POTUS).

I kept getting very flustered. I felt like everyone was looking at me (they were), and I got antsy and uncomfortable. There was something about not having the answers at the tip of my tongue in front of a jury of my peers that was making me feel like a fraud.

After it was over, my assistant, Clay, and Joe Paulsen came in to my office and sat down across from me. They told me they had ideas on how to make me feel better. I told them I was open to anything.

A few hours later, Clay and Joe came back with a questionnaire. It was huge—about 15 pages long. They told me to take it to my favorite Thai restaurant, get a glass of wine, and fill it out.

Favorite TV show, last book I read, and what I do all day—the survey was basic in many ways, but so helpful. When I realized my favorite TV show was *The Mindy Project* and the last book I had read was *Is Everybody Hanging Out Without Me?*, also by Mindy Kaling, Clay pointed out that it made me sound a little too fangirl, even if it was true and even if she was a friend.

(A perk of my job: Once, POTUS was doing an event at the Waldorf in New York, and she happened to be there at the same time. It was very hard for me to finish a book while I was deputy chief, so everyone, including Obama, had seen me carrying around *Is Everyone Hanging Out Without Me?* for weeks. After the event, I was at dinner with POTUS—when you traveled with the president, he would usually request that a couple of people have dinner with him—and Bobby Schmuck, an adviser, came over to ask if he wanted to meet Mindy. I freaked out, Mindy came over, and POTUS said something like, "Actually, the person you should really meet is Alyssa." From then on we were friends.)

Anyway, I told Clay that the book I had finished before that was *Are You There, Vodka? It's Me, Chelsea*, and he replied, "Well, he probably won't ask you both!"

I spent a lot of time thinking about my outfit. I had this great Proenza Schouler dress that I had taken to Paris Fashion Week in 2012; it was a contender, but I had worn it for everything important I had done since. There were a few other dresses, but ultimately I didn't want to worry about how to cross my legs, so I just wore regular old J.Crew from head to toe. I decided to go with my inner Diane Keaton—white collared shirt, gray sweater, red glasses. I wanted to look like someone you would want to have at a fun dinner party. I had tamed my hair per the good advice of my friend Michael Smith, whose response to hearing I had an interview was, "I'm SO proud of you! Make sure your hair isn't too big!" I did my own makeup, which was minimal because I hate how I look in makeup. The people at *Charlie Rose* gave me a little antishine and bronzer, but that was about it. They also put my hair in a good order. (Coincidentally, one of my best friends from UVM, Sam, was producing the segment, which made me feel much more at ease.)

The interview was about 75 minutes long and over before I knew it. As soon as the cameras were off, Charlie and I both checked our BlackBerries, which had been lighting up like crazy—Secretary of Health and Human Services Kathleen Sebelius had announced her resignation while we were taping. (And thank God she did it during the interview and not before—I had memorized our health-care enrollment numbers but would not have known what to say about her; I thought she was announcing the following day so hadn't prepared any talking points on it.)

I was so fucking proud of myself. Seeing myself on TV was probably one of the things I was most scared of in the world, and I was so worried about being able to talk about my accomplishments and still come off as myself, rather than some weird, scripted version of me. I kept it together until we got outside, and then Clay and Joe, who had been watching on the monitor, made me celebrate. I decided to not be too critical and take their word for it. I had told the story of my time with Barack Obama, and I did it justice and enjoyed it.

The day the interview aired, DK wasn't home, so I was able to watch it by myself, though I almost didn't watch it at all—it took two glasses of wine to psych me up to turn on the TV. When I finally put it on, I watched the whole thing through my hands like it was a horror movie.

But I didn't need to; I thought I was awesome. I laughed (I was funny!), I cried (I did it!), I didn't make a mockery of Charlie's show or Obama's presidency, and that's all that mattered. The next day Gayle King called me a "badass mamba jamba" on *CBS This Morning*.

So many people reached out to me after they saw the show. An older man from the Midwest said I had restored his faith in government. A wonderful woman who heard that I got my dresses from a consignment shop offered to send me her old Oscar de la Renta gowns. (I couldn't accept them—though I wanted to—but thanked her profusely.)

About a month later, after I had left the White House, Cutter called to tell me that her friend Anne Finucane, the vice chairman of Bank of America, had seen the interview and asked her to introduce us.

I met Anne for tea, and she asked me about the White House and what I wanted to do for my next phase. I was pretty honest and said I had no idea. She said that I was young enough to have another big adventure and not to worry if it was a disaster, which was very reassuring (but also not). She said she would keep me in mind if she heard of anything and to keep in touch.

A few weeks passed and Anne texted me from Cannes. "I am with Shane Smith, Bono, and the Edge right now," she said. I thought this was a joke that would end with a priest and a rabbi. "You need to meet Shane Smith."

A month or so later, I went to the VICE offices in Williamsburg, Brooklyn. This was harder than it sounds; I showed up at two different entrances, both of them wrong, but I did appreciate how nice the office operations team in shipping and receiving was. I finally found my way to the main door, introduced myself, and waited for someone to come get me for my meeting with Shane. Finally, the man himself came down. I joked that his being able to identify me right away probably wasn't a compliment; the lobby was full of people younger than I am. And with many more tattoos.

Two months later I accepted a job as their chief operating officer. Many of my friends (and my husband) thought I was crazy; I had never worked in media before, but even if I had, this was not just any old media company. But then again, politics isn't exactly a calm, straightforward career path, either, and I felt like I had made a real impact there. Why shouldn't I be able to do the same at VICE Media?

You leave the White House only once (usually), and that first move matters more than anything else. With that one decision, your personal stock either rises or falls. I hated this, but I kept thinking about what the men (Plouffe, Jim Messina) I'd worked with had gone on to do, and I felt like I had to make a similar statement with my new job. It would be a challenge, but part of me wanted to be reborn after tying my success to Barack Obama's for almost ten years. Going into something totally new—and something that, frankly, not many people do after they leave the White House—felt like the way to do it. Besides, the energy and youthfulness at VICE made it feel like a campaign, which was a space I was comfortable in. I also very much wanted to wear whatever I wanted to work again. It was a risky move, but so was Barack Obama running for president. Right?

CHAPTER 9

Resilience, or A "Serious" Breakdown

I felt so good going into my last day at the White House that I had not only packed my boxes and cleaned out my office but had had the folks who hang art in the West Wing prepare it for its new occupant, Pfeiffer.

This feeling did not last. When you leave the White House, your security clearance disappears. Someone comes and tells you what it means to lose your clearance, makes sure you know not to ever talk about anything classified that you've learned in your time there, and then takes your security badge and you are done.

This is the moment when it hit me.

I cried and cried. One of my favorite documentaries is *The September Issue*, about the making of the biggest issue of *Vogue* of the year. In the film, Anna Wintour talks about how her dad knew it was time to leave the London *Evening Standard*—he said it was because he had started getting angry. I had started getting angry. For many months, I knew it was probably time to go.

But for nearly a decade, my identity, rightly or wrongly, had been defined by the man I worked for. I knew who I was in terms of the structure of the office, and I had a good idea of what people outside the building thought of me—hard-working, critical-thinking, gets-to-yes, keeps her head down, team player, a little sensitive. That is who I was, and it felt OK to hook my identity to that because I had worked so hard to get there and stay there. And because the man I worked for was the president of the United States.

As I was trying and failing to pull myself together, I looked at the security guy and said, "I'm sure this happens a lot?"

It doesn't.

Just as I was finally calming down, the vice president came in to say good-bye. I love that guy. More tears. (From him, too!) When I eventually tried to make a break for it, Anita and Ferial came to get me for the good-bye toast in the Oval Office. I'm sure you think I'm being really douchey, but in many ways everyone hates these. Having POTUS say good-bye to you in the Oval is a once-in-a-lifetime experience—an honor—but you are also on display while you choke back tears and try to slam champagne and a chocolate-covered strawberry without getting seeds stuck in your teeth.

But obviously if POTUS didn't do it, you would be bummed. No winning.

POTUS gave me a painting of a landscape in Iowa (it is one of the first things you will see when you walk into our condo; I am always too happy to explain where it came from), and when we went outside into the beautiful May evening on the lawn, the whole gang was there. Even Favs and Plouffe, who had left the year before, were back for it.

As this was happening, I realized and actually said out loud that I loved everyone and that I didn't know if I was ready to be emotionally independent from them. I am confident in my ability to do work and adapt, but I was not confident in my ability to support myself. Many people go through this after a long-term relationship breaks up—*I think you're an amazing person, and I only hope for the best for you! I just need some time apart!*—and my leaving the White House was kind of like that. I was worried that I had spent so many years with this group of people, this dysfunctional but fiercely protective family, that I would be bereft of company. Any major, life-changing moment I'd had as an adult had been with them. (And often because of them.) Some losing, more winning, getting married. They knew it all and still loved me (usually).

The time came to put all my boxes in my car and drive away. You accumulate a lot over eight years; after Pfeiffer helped me put everything in my car, it looked, and felt, a lot like when I was leaving for college. Bags of shoes, photos, jackets, some state dinner dresses I had changed out of in my office and never taken home. Plus, Pfeiffer and I had a special relationship; we were the same age and had been through it all, from Chicago to now, together. We had seen each other grow up.

The send-off was like the scene from *90210* when Brenda leaves for London and says good-bye to Dylan: We told each other we were best friends for life and cried and cried and cried some more. The only thing I could do was get into the Ford Escape and drive through the gates of the White House and onto Pennsylvania Avenue one last time, listening to Led Zeppelin as loudly as I could.

I was so sad, but I didn't have time to be: I was booked for three parties in four days. I very briefly considered bailing on mine and Kathy's going-away party that night—"Alyssa and Kathy's Last-Chance Dance"—because I didn't want to get off the couch. (It's a good thing that I managed it, though, because we had pigs in a blanket, and I will always remember Mindy saying, "Is that the national security adviser dropping it like it's hot?")

The next day, I was so hung over that David had to go to Five Guys to get me a cheeseburger and fries, but I had to rally because I was going to the White House Correspondents' Dinner. I had an invite to the *Vanity Fair* party, but I absolutely could not go. (Though I didn't miss Obama's performance: "Just last month, a wonderful story—an American won the Boston Marathon for the first time in 30 years. Which was inspiring, and only fair, since a Kenyan has been president for the last six!")

That Monday, I went to the Met Ball as a guest of Anna Wintour, who invited me when she heard my White House departure date was May 2. I had a vintage Valentino dress that I got at my consignment shop (and had altered to fit my butt). When I went to get my makeup done at Barneys, they politely asked if I wanted my hair done as well. I told them I'd had my hair done already, and they fixed it.

On Tuesday, I crashed. Not like I got wasted at the Met

Ball—though I was part of a very early set of arrivals, 5:45 PM, and they didn't serve food at the cocktail hour—but I got depressed. The years of adrenaline and purpose from the White House bottomed out faster than you can say "*House Hunters* marathon."

I wasn't just eating dry cereal out of the box and crying. I took meetings. I helped out at the DNC and served on the technical advisory group that selected Philly for the 2016 convention. I was appointed to boards: the University of Wisconsin Board of Visitors, the John F. Kennedy Center for the Performing Arts Board of Trustees, HeadCount. I became a contributing editor at *Marie Claire*. I had been on *Charlie Rose* right before I left, and because of that I was able to take even more meetings. I got to have dinner with Bob Weir, the guitarist for the Grateful Dead, and talk about digitizing folk music with Mickey Hart, one of the drummers for the band.

Even with all that, I felt like shit. I was totally lost. I had no idea who I was or what I was going to do. On days when I didn't have plans, I would wake up, eat breakfast, watch TV, and go back to sleep; sometimes I would get dressed right before David came home from work so he wouldn't know I had been sleeping in the middle of the day. When you go from checking your BlackBerry 500 times a day, needing to be available and responsive 24/7, to being able to sleep until 8:00 AM, wake up, have a leisurely breakfast, and do whatever you want—it sounds awesome, but you also wonder why no one is calling you. Weren't you invaluable? Irreplaceable?

We are all replaceable. Life goes on, but that doesn't mean it feels good.

To add insult to injury, about two months after I left, a reporter wrote a feature for *Politico* in which my becoming a contributing editor at *Marie Claire* was the lede—and she wasn't saying the development was part of an exciting trend of women's magazines covering more politics and international news. She quoted my press release about the job, where I said I appreciated *Marie Claire*'s fashion editorial as well as its coverage of global women's issues, before arguing that while these two aims should be mutually exclusive, for women in power, they can't be. In other words, any time someone like me expresses interest in beautiful clothes, or celebrities, or whatever, it doesn't indicate that I have a multifaceted personality with a healthy balance between light, fun hobbies and intellectual, political, and professional concerns—no, this reporter said, it means I have been squashed under the thumb of the patriarchy.

This pretty much sums it up:

For nine years, Mastromonaco guided Obama's political trajectory behind the scenes. In 2011, the *New Republic* listed her as one of "Washington's Most Powerful, Least Famous People"; according to POLITICO, she "managed nearly every aspect of Obama's political rise." But even as she guided the life of the man running the most powerful country in the world, she remained typecast in the media in the two (very contradictory) roles

allowed for women in public life: at once a Machiavel-
lian maneuverer and a cupcake-eating cheerleader.

She went on to say that a *New York Times* profile of me
was insulting both because it mentioned the fact that my
hair had turned prematurely gray so I dye it (it's true) and
because it described me as being powerful.

I knew she was wrong, but at the same time, because I had
lost my purpose, it also felt like I'd made a huge mistake.
Had I thrown away everything that could or would make my
life meaningful?

I wrote an op-ed in response, which, because I was truly
furious, my friend Lea had to make readable. I argued that
modern women see no contradiction in being both informed
and fashionable (and that men's magazines don't get much
grief for running photos of women in bikinis alongside lengthy
reportage). It ran in the *Washington Post*. I had spent so much
time trying to keep myself (and my opinions) out of the public
eye while I worked for Obama that I was incredibly nervous,
but I couldn't let her piece go unanswered. She was dismissing
my choices for not being "serious" enough. But what is "serious" enough? If she had known I was also working with the
DNC, or HeadCount, would that have changed her mind?

■　■　■

Honestly, who cares? Between *Charlie Rose* and the op-ed, I
was more visible than I had been in years, and I was actually
proud. I had been so deathly afraid of having a profile, and of
saying something that might cause trouble for POTUS, that

I had assumed there was no such thing as good publicity. But in the meantime, I had learned the boundaries of what I did and didn't want to say. I got better at talking about myself.

I took even more meetings. If I had focused and gotten my shit together, I might have made better use of it all, but I was so overwhelmed that I often felt like I showed up to the meetings and just sat there and blinked.

I mentioned before that Anne Finucane, the vice chairman at Bank of America, had seen my *Charlie Rose* interview and asked Cutter to introduce us. Even though she eventually got me a job, when I went to meet her for tea, I was really intimidated, and I didn't feel like I was being the best version of myself. She was the one who wanted to meet with me—I should have strutted in there and dazzled her with my deep knowledge of the recession and the debt ceiling—but I felt like I wasn't performing. Halfway through our conversation, she stopped and said, "I want you to come work for me, but I don't think that's right for you right now. Let me help you find what is."

I had read about Shane Smith, seen VICE in our Situation Room news clips, and watched the show on HBO. When we set up our meeting, I knew they were based in Brooklyn and imagined the office populated with tattooed skateboarders who talked about music I'd never heard of. And that's about it.

.   .   .

Around the same time, I signed my book deal. I was still thinking about VICE, but while I mulled it over, writing a book felt like something that made sense—many people who leave the White House write books, and it brings them glory and gravitas, and everyone goes to the book party and it's a great time of rehashing your greatest moments. Reggie Love's and Axelrod's books were going to come out the next year, and Plouffe's was published soon after the 2008 campaign. There wasn't really a woman from the White House who'd written the kind of thing I envisioned, but I had a clear enough idea of what I wanted to do that it wasn't daunting.

The idea was an advice book/memoir geared toward women between the ages of about 15 and 25. Knowing Mindy made me think there should be something similar to her books, but for politics; although mine wouldn't be as funny, I hoped it could help women see themselves working in government. It wouldn't be chronological—because to me chronology seemed too much like you were trying to leave your legacy—but instead would be organized by qualities that have helped me in my career: leadership, preparedness, resilience, etc. It was going to be great. I had all these funny stories and important lessons that I was going to impart to my legions of readers, who would be so inspired by my story of hard work and tampons that they would be firing up their laptops to apply for Senate internships in no time. I finally had something to hang my hat on after months when there was not a single hat rack to be found.

A friend was writing her book as I was trying to write mine, and I would talk to her about it a lot. Soon, six months had gone by, and talking to my friend was the extent of the work

I'd done. Nothing. I began to worry that agreeing to do it at all had been an act of hubris. Being a writer is a profession—just like being a veterinarian, lawyer, or ballerina. I couldn't wake up one morning and be a ballerina. Why did I believe I could wake up one morning and write a book?

Eventually I tried to come up with a more detailed outline than what I'd turned in to the publisher, and it made me feel even worse. I realized how uncomfortable I was with talking about the White House and the president. I didn't want to tell anyone else's story—it wasn't my place—so every anecdote I wanted to include, I ended up designating as "somebody else's" and putting it in the NO pile. I would watch old campaign videos to get myself psyched up, but they just filled me with dread.

By early September 2014, I had written an introduction and a first chapter. I was feeling a little better, but still—not great. It was OK, though, because all I needed was to get it done so that it could come out in the spring of 2016—the last graduation season when Obama would still be in office. I had plenty of time.

* * *

Meanwhile, I had begun to negotiate my contract with VICE, and here, too, I was out of my depth. I had only really worked on campaigns and in the government, both of which have transparent pay scales; salaries are publicly disclosed and reported in the *Washington Post* every July 1. You know what every single person in the White House makes. I had even more insight because I managed the salaries.

So I was completely unprepared to negotiate my offer at a private company—it didn't even really occur to me that it would be different. Since VICE had this cool-kid reputation, I didn't want to roll in with my big-deal DC lawyer, Bob Barnett, who had negotiated my book deal. Against the advice of DK, who knows what he is talking about, I did it myself, with some solid input from Kathy Ruemmler.

Out of left field, VICE asked me what I thought I should make. If anyone ever asks you this—and they probably will—do not give a number. Sometimes employers will ask what your current salary is, and unfortunately, you cannot fib there; if they call your reference and it's your boss, they could find out what you're making now and know you've lied, which looks so much worse than working for a lower-than-average paycheck. But if anyone asks you to tell them what you want, you should respond as follows: "I'm sure there's a salary band for the position, and my hope would be to come in at the high end of that."

I, however, sat down and did what I thought was thoughtful and considered math: I incorporated what I could expect to bring in through fees for speaking events, what I had made working in the government, my experience level, and what other companies had floated as salaries to me when I met with them. I came up with a number, and I sent it to VICE.

I'll say it again: Don't do this!!!!! When they came back with less than what I'd asked for, instead of chalking it up to negotiation tactics and calling Bob, I was shocked. All my bros from the White House didn't seem to run into this issue when they got their first jobs post–White House; as far as I knew, they'd just gotten their offers and accepted. (This is probably not what happened.) At the time, I don't think I realized my confidence was still simmering on low. Maybe I wasn't who I thought I was? I talked them up a bit and accepted the job.

Two months later, I showed up for my first day—January 5, 2015—and it was immediately clear that I was in for a culture shock. VICE is, as Shane Smith told the *New York Times* for the article that ran about my move, "craz[y]" and "freaky"—a huge place with hundreds of people. Many have tattoos, fewer are skateboarders; there were a lot of ripped jeans and very purposeful hairstyles. Some crop tops, even in January. The office sees a huge turnover of business-looking people, as well as celebrities, every day; no one cared—or even noticed—when I walked into the cavernous space on North 11th Street where the Brooklyn office was located at the time. Most people were typing intensely on MacBooks, not looking up or talking, even though they were all sitting at communal tables. It would take me maybe longer than it should have to realize that they weren't cold or rude—they were just concentrating on writing.

After a week or so, I was able to make some observations: (1) This was the first time ever that I had been the oldest person in the room. (2) This was the first time in maybe 12 years that I had been "the new person"; I even had to ask where the bathroom was. (3) I basically knew nothing about how media companies operate. (4) This was going to be much harder than I had expected.

Trying to write a book reflecting on the successes and lessons of your career is very hard when you genuinely feel like a fraud who hasn't learned from any of her past mistakes. In my experience, it is, in fact, impossible.

Months passed, and almost every day I thought about the book. I had convinced David to move to New York with promises of how fun our life would be there, but the transition was a total disaster: The sale of our Georgetown place fell through at the last minute. We bought a condo in Tribeca only to learn that construction was a year behind schedule; we had to live in short-term rentals until it was finished. The first place I found online—on Greene Street in SoHo—turned out to be a scam: I went on StreetEasy and saw that the building was owned by someone who was not the person I had been communicating with, and I had already paid a deposit and the first month's rent. One of the places we ended up staying in Williamsburg had pleather couches. Often, the apartments were in crappy new buildings where recent college graduates—who, famously, like to party—lived. At one point during this saga, when it was particularly chaotic, David said to me, "I did not achieve in my life to live with twenty-two-year-olds." I had failed at leaving the White House and had no one to blame but myself.

At least a few times a week I would open up my computer—the one David bought me when I got the book deal—and stare at it. Every morning at 5:30 AM an Outlook reminder went off, telling me to get up and write my book. I would get out of bed and sit on a pleather couch and not write it.

I convinced myself that I just needed to feel settled—to be "home"—and the words would come. But when we finally moved into our place in Tribeca—our home—they didn't. I challenged myself to dedicate all day to the book every Sunday, and I would go down the street to Kaffe 1668 and sit and write. After nine Sundays dedicated to this, I had two tiny chapters.

By April 2016—almost two years since I'd gotten the deal—I had pretty much decided to give up. I just hadn't told anyone else.

※ ※ ※

In the months leading up to this moment, VICE had been in collective bargaining contract negotiations. The August before, the editorial team had voted to unionize, and I had been put in charge of the negotiation process for the management side, which is kind of hilarious and horrible when you think about it—a lifelong active Democrat negotiating against the worker. (I guess the flip-side rationale was that I was familiar with labor unions.) This was hard for me to resolve, especially because I was someone who was relatively new to a company full of fiercely loyal employees; they didn't know me, or have a reason to trust me, at all. I hit an emotional rock bottom. The night after a particularly brutal, hours-long bargaining session, I was drinking wine on the floor of my bathroom. My cat has severe anxiety, and he wouldn't come out, so I just stayed in there.

I began suffering from debilitating stomach pains, and after two trips to urgent care and a week of freaking out on WebMD, I went to a doctor.

He asked a hundred questions about my life—eating habits, family history, sleep patterns. One of the last ones was, "Do you drink alcohol?" I said yes.

"How is that possible?" he asked. "It must kill your stomach."

"It's actually the only thing that makes me feel better," I said.

Aha. He went straight for the jugular. He asked about my job, and I melted into tears right there in my hospital gown. Not heaving, sobbing tears, but the tears actresses aim for in movies. Streaming out of the corners of my eyes. His theory was that my intense stomach pains weren't the result of giardia from Mexican takeout (my WebMD diagnosis) or IBS or cancer (other WebMD diagnoses) but from anxiety and depression.

I couldn't believe it. I would never look in the mirror and think I was seeing someone depressed. And anxiety? After six and a half years in the White House, *working in media* was giving me anxiety?

The doctor and I talked about how the White House was probably exhausting, and difficult, but in a way, shockingly, controlled for me. I was used to that kind of environment because I am a planner, but much of what happens in media evades planning—you never know when a story will break, or when someone will have a great idea that a team needs to start working on now. The theory was that the chaos at VICE and my inability to wrangle it were literally destroying my insides. (This doctor is a gastroenterologist and not a therapist, just to be clear, but I would support his taking up a side gig if the stomach stuff doesn't work out.)

He gave me a prescription for Zoloft. I didn't really want to take medication, but I needed something, and within 48 hours my stomach pains were gone. I felt like an entirely new person.

The union negotiations wrapped up shortly after I told myself that I would abandon the book, and despite feeling dejected that I was on the verge of giving up on this project, the vibe around the office got much lighter. (The editorial team all got big raises, among other things.) I didn't feel like everyone hated me anymore; in fact, I started to make some friends.

One of the good things about the process was that it allowed me to get to know a handful of employees much better. Lauren Oyler represented the women's vertical site, Broadly, at the bargaining table, and I had read what she'd been writing for months. Her arguments were always compelling, and she was always working; I began to think she might be able to help me with the book. I needed structure and perspective pretty desperately. Also, given the target audience, I really wanted a millennial POV.

A little more than a month after negotiations ended, we worked together on something else, and I got to know her more. She was smart and no bullshit and just straight-up impressive. I identified her as my savior.

It was July at this point, and I was at a shit-or-get-off-the-pot moment with this damn book.

Since her name is on the book, you know how this ends. She helped me focus, gave me direction, was critical but kind, and most importantly reminded me why doing this mattered.

She also assuaged my fears that this was a self-aggrandizing *I'm the Best and Only Champion of Politics* type of memoir.

One of the good things about being resilient is that, when you're forced to veer off course, you pick up skills you didn't realize you needed. That was probably the most I've ever struggled professionally, but I'm still here. Being resilient means being honest: You have to admit when you're struggling. Usually, someone will help you.

(Hi, it's me, Lauren, writing to you from my kitchen table in Brooklyn. I feel strange letting a string of compliments about me into the book, but there needs to be a resolution to this story, and I am, weirdly or not, the resolution! If you would like to know my personal favorite part of the book, it's when Obama walks in on Alyssa doing sit-ups in her office during a Senate Voterama and goes, "Good for you.")

CHAPTER 10

Kindness, or A Spirit Soars over Denali

When I was 18 and working at Kilmer's IGA in Rhinebeck, I took an afternoon shift on prom day. Most of the other checkers were off getting ready, but I agreed to work the latest shift because my hair was really short and I wasn't having it done. I was about to close out my register when Natalie Merchant, the lead singer of 10,000 Maniacs, and Michael Stipe, from R.E.M., walked in.

Natalie lived down the road, in Rhinecliff, and she came to Kilmer's often; she was probably the first person I ever saw use recyclable grocery bags. She was very friendly and asked where all the other girls were. I told her it was prom night and that as soon as I rang her up, I was going to leave and put my dress on, too. (It was a very plain little black dress—a real departure from the bugle beads and sequins I had worn the year before.) She asked where the dance was, and I told her.

About five hours later, slow dances to All-4-One's "I Swear" at Valeur Mansion on River Road screeched to a halt and we were treated to an impromptu performance by Natalie

215

Merchant, who stopped by to say hello. She welcomed all the girls who were in the choir to join her. This was long before social media gave people instant credit for acts of goodwill— she just did it because she was a member of the community and thought it might mean something to us.

It did. For one, because she was a notoriously private person—when you saw her in town, you didn't fawn over her or ask for an autograph—but also because she didn't stop by because we were the kids of important or famous people. We were the kids who scooped her ice cream and packed her grocery bags.

*　*　*

There are certain lessons you pick up gradually as you go, letting them accumulate after a series of similar mistakes or experiences until you finally realize you've been a fool all along. And then there are the lessons that are so massive they smack you in the face—you don't reflect on a period of your life and realize, "Oh, I learned something then"; you know it's happening when it's happening. The importance of kindness—which extends far beyond "please," "thank you," and "your hair doesn't look bad today"—is a combination of both: Over and over in my life, I've been bowled over by how kind people can be, and how that kindness can change your outlook. Politics is often associated with secret dealings, competition, and corruption—and those associations aren't necessarily wrong—but, fundamentally, it's also about people and personalities. Working at the White House is obviously heady, but it's also humbling—you're around the most brilliant, decorated brains in the country. They don't have to do anything for you, but they often do. If you approach it with grace—and a willingness to accept that many people know much more than you—you can walk away a much better person than you were when you came in.

When we were kicking off the transition, I made a trip to DC for a meeting with President-elect Obama, and while I was waiting for him to meet me Larry Summers, who was about to become the director of the National Economic Council, zoomed by. I had never met Larry, but before becoming part of the Obama family, he was chief economist at the World Bank and treasury secretary in the Clinton administration, so I knew who he was and felt a little starstruck. It was one of many nerdy celebrity sightings at the transition office. As he was about to turn a corner, he whirled around and asked me to get him a Diet Coke.

Just like that, my admiration turned to contempt. The gall! The nerve! The bad man! I was so offended. *Did he not know who I was?*

Well, no, he didn't. I was no one. While I had been cranking hard for years for Barack Obama and at times felt like a political veteran, I was 32 years old and looked my age only on a good day. I had packed on the pounds in Chicago, eating my fill of chicken al' diavolo and chocolate cake from Portillo's, and my cheeks were nice and full—it's entirely possible I was clocking in at around 25. If I didn't look like an intern, I certainly looked like someone who could get you a Diet Coke. Also, I was the only other person in the room.

None of this registered at the time—I was indignant at

what I perceived to be a sexist injustice against me. Would he ask *a man* to get him a soda? I begrudgingly got him a Diet Coke from the vending machine and decided to write him off forever as a douche bag. I committed to rolling my eyes (internally) every time he spoke.

Months later, we saw each other again—in a meeting in the Roosevelt Room about the economic crisis. Larry was the president's national economic adviser. Tim Geithner (secretary of the treasury), Christie Romer (chief of the Council of Economic Advisers), and Peter Orszag (director of the Office of Budget and Management) were sitting at my end of the table, along with Gibbs. The economists were talking about their alma maters (Dartmouth, William & Mary, MIT, Princeton), and Peter asked if Gibbs or I ever felt out of place because we didn't go to an Ivy League school. I could feel my face getting hot—remembering that awful day when I got skinny envelopes from Cornell, Brown, and Georgetown saying "Thanks, but no thanks."

"Well, we all ended up at the same table, didn't we?" Gibbs—who went to North Carolina State—shot back. "Seems like we got a bargain!" Um, true.

Meetings on the economic crisis—of which there were many in 2009—made me so nervous, but as a member of the president's senior staff I needed to understand what was happening, because recovery was POTUS's number one priority. Everything POTUS did—his meetings, his events, the layout of his day—was viewed through the lens of "What can we do to impact the recovery?"

These meetings were totally outside my comfort zone (I

got a B– in Econ 101). I would always panic that one day POTUS would launch into the Socratic method and randomly ask me to pontificate on TARP (I will save you the Googling: Troubled Asset Relief Program) or quantitative easing (go ahead and Google this one—it's good for you). I would break into a literal sweat just walking into the room.

Because it was my responsibility to learn everything I possibly could, when people used a term I didn't know the meaning of I would write it down to research, quietly and without embarrassing myself, later. During this particular meeting, I was sitting next to Larry, and I guess he saw my list of terms to search and articles to read; this time, it was focused on the shadow banking system, debt deflation, and subprime loans.

In the middle of the meeting, he whispered, "Come up to my office after this."

The jig was up. He knew I was a fraud. Or worse—just not that smart.

After the meeting, I followed him upstairs, where he asked about my list. As embarrassing as it was, I decided to just be honest and tell him. I was a moron! It was about to be all out in the open. Could I get him another Diet Coke?

But to my surprise—since I'd labeled him a jerk—he was totally nice. "Well, if you knew everything I knew," he asked, "what good would I be?" He took about an hour to explain very complicated concepts to me, and he suggested some articles that would help me get up to speed.

I'm sure he doesn't remember doing it, because he wasn't trying to be extraordinary—he was just being kind. But because of that one gesture, I would always ask Larry questions when I had them, and when, as part of my job as deputy chief four years later, I had to screen candidates for chairman of the Federal Reserve, I wasn't a total disaster. When I sat with POTUS to do the interviews—Larry himself withdrew from the final round—I held my own, and I didn't sweat through my dress worrying I might get caught up in a conversation I knew nothing about.

Larry taught me two very important lessons. The first: Never judge a book by its cover (or the articles written about it). The second: Always make time to help a gal out. Kindness—you can call it generosity, or goodwill—really means something.

❊ ❊ ❊

Right after Hurricane Katrina in 2005, the *Washington Post* ran a story about how all the dogs that had been rescued from the storm were being adopted, but the cats were being euthanized. It featured a picture of this giant calico Persian named Tommy who had been evacuated from New Orleans and found his way up to the Persian Rescue of Virginia. I had always wanted to get a cat, and I felt like this was my moment.

I called the rescuer, Margaret, and asked about Tommy. I said I was interested in him; she told me that he took up the space of four cats and that if someone didn't take him this week he would probably be put down.

The rescue was only about a 50-minute drive away, but I was afraid to go to the hinterlands of Virginia by myself, so I asked my friend David Wade to come with me. I figured

Margaret had to be joking about how big he was. I mean, four cats?

It was the weirdest experience ever. Margaret ran the rescue out of her condo, though it was clean and she clearly cared for all the cats very well. She brought Tommy to the kitchen and put him on the table. He yawned, stretched out to cover basically the entire thing, and closed his eyes but didn't fall asleep—it was like he was meditating. Margaret had an Irish brogue and told us Tommy could sense when she was about to get her period. We asked no more questions. He was handsome and calm and I knew we were meant to be.

Margaret put Tommy in a dog crate (he weighed 23 pounds—the size of three small cats), and Wade and I put him in the back of my Saab and drove back to the Hill. The entire ride back, Wade was in the front seat whispering "You're free!" to Tommy.

That night, I couldn't sleep—it was like having a raccoon in the house. I could see his tail whipping across the front of my bed and hear him sniffing around; he attacked his litter box with a ferocity I did not know domesticated house cats could have. (This did not temper itself over the years.) When he peed, he would wake me up because it was so loud. When I tried to talk to him or pet him, he would hide under the green armchair my parents bought right after they were married in 1974.

This was not sustainable. I called Possum.

Possum was also a cat lover, and he had two of his own. I told him that I had adopted Tommy and changed his name to Shrummie—after Bob Shrum, the Democratic political strategist whom I'd spent a fair amount of time with on the Kerry campaign; I just thought he was so lovely that I would name a cat after him one day. Shrummie was hiding under an old chair and wouldn't come out, and I needed Possum's help.

Pete Rouse, the man who had seen a Senate majority leader through the impeachment of a president, came over, sat down cross-legged in his cowboy boots and jeans on the creaky wooden floor in my little apartment and spent approximately five minutes coaxing Shrummie out from under the chair. I couldn't believe it.

* * *

A few months earlier, my boyfriend Marv and I had broken up. We had dated for almost six years, and I loved him very much—he was my best friend—but we both knew something wasn't right and hadn't been for a while. We lived down the street from each other for years. He was still working for Kerry—how we met—but had lots of friends in the Obama office. We broke up during our lunch break on the day the Vatican sent the white smoke out of the chimney to signify they had chosen a new pope. I was crying on the sidewalk and told Marv through my tears, "People must think I'm really upset about the new pontiff."

After our conversation, I went back to the office with red, puffy eyes. When Anita (Decker Breckenridge—then our downstate Illinois director) called me to talk about Obama's next trip, she could tell I was upset. I told her what had happened, and she confessed she was going through the same thing. We were friendly before, but this made us sisters-in-arms.

A few weeks later, she suggested we give match.com a whirl. I was pretty lonely at that point; the DC political community is small, and when people heard Marv—who is about six feet eight inches and was a hot commodity—and I had broken up, they would throw parties and invite basically everyone I knew except me, because all the girls wanted to date him. In 2005, Match was sort of the preeminent dating website, and this was my first foray into online anything.

Cara helped me write my profile over pad thai and cocktails, and I posted it and waited. We trolled prospects and were kind of unimpressed; preempting Tinder by several years, we agreed that anyone who lived in Virginia was a No. This is simple, DC-resident prejudice and not right, but it's where I was at age 30.

About a week went by before Anita and I regrouped to discuss our progress. She asked how many "winks" I'd gotten.

"Um, what's a wink?" I replied. I checked my profile—nothing. I clicked through the site and realized "winks" came from guys who thought your profile/photo were cute. Anita had 30. I had none.

COME ON.

I became overwhelmed with emotion and started to cry at my desk. Not ugly crying—more like a string of single tears—but crying nonetheless. Any postbreakup fear that I might die alone was being confirmed. My lifelong unhappiness was cemented after five days on match.com.

Possum came over to talk about something else and saw I was crying. I'm kind of an open book—it's not that I lack boundaries, but I don't think emotions are something to be ashamed of—so I told him what was wrong. This meant explaining what exactly match.com was and why "winks" mattered. He grumbled. "I don't understand this," he said, and walked away. Possum does not like having his personal space violated, and I worried for a minute that I had been a little extreme.

The next day I came into the office and there was a card on my desk. Inside was a cat winking and the message, "This guy will wink at you."

＊　＊　＊

I always say that if it weren't for Shrummie, David and I probably never would have gotten married. In the middle of our relationship, I had to go on a long trip to Asia with POTUS. DK asked who took care of Shrummie when I went away; I told him about this pet-sitting service, FurPals, that I used.

Although many women would be put off by the "Rent, don't own" and "Never get married" aspects of David's personal philosophy, I didn't get that far, because the "No pets" one seemed like the first deal breaker for me in a life partner. But in a fairly shocking move, he offered to have Shrummie come stay with him instead. He had met Shrummie a few times, and because Shrummie likes dudes best, he cuddled up to David immediately. Nevertheless, Shrummie was about 13 at this point, and although he'd shed a solid eight pounds with the help of Science Diet cat food, he still had his quirks (and fur that shed like crazy).

While I was in Asia, David would write me notes from Shrummie about how much fun he was having at "Uncle David's"; he knew he was naughty to wake Uncle David up at 3:00 AM for snacks, but good old Uncle David got out of bed to give him food anyway. From there, David's relationship with Shrummie grew. They became best friends, and this was my first indicator that maybe David's policy on bachelorhood wasn't as strict as I'd thought.

The week after David and I got married, we awoke on Thanksgiving morning in Rhinebeck to a paralyzed Shrummie—he couldn't use his hind legs. We were supposed to be having dinner with Cara, her husband, and some other people to celebrate our nuptials, but I was so upset about Shrummie that instead of a festive meal at Le Petit Bistro, everyone came to the house for pizza and beer.

Shrummie's legs eventually started working again, but he was still really off. We left Rhinebeck around 9:00 PM to get him back to more familiar surroundings in Georgetown, and for the next few weeks, he wasn't right. He didn't eat and was in and out of the animal hospital.

Meanwhile, Nelson Mandela passed away, and it was my job to oversee the presidential delegation for the funeral. For someone like Mandela, this meant former presidents and first ladies. With more than 300 current and former heads of state coming, the South African government was totally in over their heads, and the trip was extremely complicated to plan. We were used to hosting and planning international summits at the White House and had the infrastructure to support them, but it was very unclear if the South African government did. The arrival of each DV could have taken more than three hours if not done properly.

The day I was getting ready to leave for Pretoria, Shrummie was really off. We took him back to the animal hospital, and I was beside myself that I had to leave. I was beyond tears; I couldn't eat. He had been tested for everything, from heart disease to pancreatic cancer, but the vet had no answers. I lost my shit—started to get really emotional—and tried to explain that I needed to leave for Nelson Mandela's funeral in a few hours so we really had to know what was wrong right then.

This is not the kind of thing you often hear working at an animal hospital, even in DC, I imagine. The vet gave me a look like I was a freedom fighter. "It's not like we were friends," I said. "It's my job." I sounded like I needed a hospital myself.

We took Shrummie home and were told to monitor his appetite, which is a key indicator (along with how many times they poop every day) of a cat's health. I headed to Andrews Air Force Base a few hours later.

When I got to AF1, President George W. Bush and Laura Bush were already on board, as was Secretary Clinton. After spending so many years traveling together, I had a nice rapport with the secretary, but I had never met Bush 43 or Mrs. Bush before (though I enjoyed her book very much and had always heard she was nice and laid-back).

"There she is! The married lady!" Secretary Clinton said from the AF1 conference room. President Bush remarked that I would probably rather be on a honeymoon than on my way to what was bound to be a shitshow in South Africa.

For some reason—I plead exhaustion, and the anxious kind of grief that I was experiencing, where you sort of know something bad is going to happen but you think you can stop it—I started telling President Bush about Shrummie. I caught myself when I started explaining the cat's "inappetence" and went back to my seat to start working on getting our Secret Service weapons into South Africa. The South African government had detained them at the airport, and we were not going to get off AF1 in Johannesburg if our protection didn't have guns.

Eventually everyone left the conference room and went to sleep, and I went back to my seat to monitor updates from our advance team on the ground. They were making little progress, but David was also sending me videos of Shrummie eating from a smorgasbord of Fancy Feast, and I felt a little better. A few hours later, President Bush came back to my cabin to ask how things were on the ground in South Africa, and how my cat was.

When I got home from South Africa two days later, Shrummie was doing OK, not great. We brought him back from the animal hospital, and out of nowhere he stopped walking again.

Late that night, we were at the animal hospital, our second home. The vet there thought—again—that Shrummie had pancreatic cancer, but that diagnosis made no sense.

Finally, at like 9:30 or something, a nice doctor pulled us aside and said she thought his problem might be neurological. There was this great neurosurgeon, Dr. Lauren Talarico, out in Virginia who might be able to help us.

The nurse called ahead, and Dr. Talarico met us sometime after 11:00 PM. She diagnosed Shrummie with a fibrocartilaginous embolism (FCE)—essentially a blockage in the spine that affects the hind limbs. She had him stay overnight—she referred to his cage as a "condo"—and said she would do an MRI to confirm and call us in the morning.

David and I went home and made a frozen pizza; it was the first time I had really eaten in weeks. I finally felt like I had someone on my side who was going to figure out, for better or worse, what was wrong. She texted me later—"Oh, we got this," I think she said—and was extremely kind.

Meanwhile—meanwhile!—our honeymoon was looming ever closer, and I got an email from the concierge at Kauri Cliffs, New Zealand, about David's tee times and my spa appointments.

When I showed David the email—not saying anything but kind of getting a sinking feeling in my stomach about the fact that I was about to go on a beautiful vacation to the Southern Hemisphere—he looked at me and said, "We aren't going." And so instead of golfing and getting massages at the edge of the world, we spent Christmas taking Shrummie for physical therapy and acupuncture. You know you've married the right person when you agree, without argument or discussion, on the decision to cancel a two-week, fully paid honeymoon so you can stay home and start your cat on intensive medical treatment. Possum told me that his cats, Moose and Buster, were saying prayers for Shrummie. Maybe it was ridiculous, but it felt like what we had to do.

I didn't realize what an important part of my life Shrummie was until he got sick. As I had moved around the country, he was the constant; he made all the random apartments I'd lived in feel like home. When I was upset or sick, he slept right next to me and wouldn't move. Even when work was shitty, you couldn't help but lighten up when he would stand at the front door waiting for you to get home so he could lead you to the cabinet with his food. He had many nicknames: Shrum, Shrummington, Shrumpkins, Porchetta, Porky Monkey Butt, and his physical therapy alter ego, Mr. Boods.

Shrummie rarely meowed, let alone hissed, but Mr. Boods would hiss at everyone at SouthPaws (though he never bit or swatted at anyone). When he walked through the PT obstacle course and hopped over hurdles, he would hiss like a tennis player grunting to get her best serve.

By this time, I was waiting for my last day at the White House to come. This is going to sound silly, but the joy his hissing brought me put that in perspective: Every one of his doctors—and especially Dr. Talarico (I am now the godmother to her daughter, Gigi)—was so kind, so invested in his recovery. Something about the entire process made me feel that either at the White House or not, I would be OK. I would have a purpose. Plus, the White House team was able and willing to arrange meetings so I would have time to go back home to Georgetown for an hour every day to give Shrummie his meds and do some quick midday physical therapy. I was never made to feel bad about it, or like a crazy cat lady. Eventually, Shrummie regained full mobility in his hind legs.

* * *

About a year after I left the White House, David and I decided to go on vacation from Williamsburg, where we were living in the horrible rentals. We never left Shrummie behind anymore—and he had been a little sleepy for a few days—so we rented a cottage out near North Fork on Long Island so we could bring him with us.

I didn't think too much of it, but we had only been gone for a few days when he seemed to get a little worse. He looked like he was dizzy—his head was sort of bobbing around—and he wasn't eating. He was actually sleeping in front of his dish, which was really odd. I asked David if we could bring Shrummie to Virginia to see Dr. Talarico, the neurosurgeon who'd helped him before; I knew that no matter what was wrong, we would figure it out there. I called her up, and she said they would start prepping "Shrummie's suite."

We drove back home to the city to unload some stuff and were planning to get right back on the road to Virginia. When we pulled into our parking space at our apartment, Shrummie started to have a seizure.

We took him straight to his vet in Tribeca—wrapped in his favorite blanket—but I knew this was it. He had fought the good fight, but I had vowed to never keep him around just for us. In his bag, I had hidden a very sweet ceramic-and-cork urn that I'd had made months earlier. Back when he first got sick, I had done a lot of late-night Internet searching and read on some message boards that if your pet is ill, you should get the urn for his ashes made in advance because you won't have the emotional fortitude to do it when the time comes. This is good advice (and a hat tip to preparedness).

I walked into the vet while David tried to park. They did a quick exam and confirmed that Shrummie was quite sick. I told them I thought it was time to put him down; David came in and we said good-bye.

When we got home, I was devastated—just empty. Everything made me tear up. I emailed Anita, who was in Alaska with POTUS. Her dog, Jonas, had gotten cancer and died a couple of months earlier, and I'd promised to let her know about Shrummie when the time came.

About 30 minutes later, I got a call from a strange number on my phone. VICE had a journalist detained in Turkey, so I figured it would be about him and answered, choking back tears.

"Ms. Mastromonaco, this is the Air Force One operator. We miss you up here! Are you available for a call from the president?"

Before I registered what was happening, I was on the phone with POTUS. "I heard we lost Shrummie today," he said. "There are a lot of sad faces up here on Air Force One right now. You should know—I'm pretty sure we saw his spirit up here over Denali."

Forget about me—that call meant so much to David,

who, by this time, loved Shrummie as much as I did, if not more. David could hear POTUS through my phone, and he teared up, too.

Having been with POTUS when he made calls like this one, I knew how hard it was. So many of the calls the president has to make are really sad—calls to parents who have lost their children serving in Iraq or Afghanistan, parents whose children were murdered or kidnapped—and in the grand scheme of things I knew that I did not rank. Barack Obama, graduate of Columbia University and Harvard Law School, broker of normalized relations between the United States and Cuba, and the nation's first black president, does not have time to call a 39-year-old woman to offer his condolences for the loss of her cat. It's bordering on an episode of *Broad City*.

I said something like, "I really appreciate this call. I know this is awful."

"He's been around since the beginning," he replied.

Later that week, I got a note from Possum saying that Shrummie had had a great life with us and had loved me very much. A month later, we rescued a crazy white Persian cat—he is older and I'm pretty sure he has an anxiety disorder—and named him Petey.

Kindness often exists on a smaller scale than the grand gestures popular on social media would have you believe. Though anonymously paying off someone's student loans or giving a waitress a $5,000 tip are amazing acts of goodwill, things like being willing to cut someone some slack, or making a thoughtful phone call, can help another person so much.

Maybe this all sounds cheesy to you. Maybe you're feeling secondhand embarrassment that Barack Obama called me to say he saw the spirit of my dead cat soaring over a mountain. Maybe you think I'm a spoiled baby—that there are real problems in the world and instead of dissecting them and advocating on behalf of them, I decided to end my book with a story about how much I love cats. (Shortly after we adopted Petey, I fell in love with another white Persian. We named her Bunny but call her BunBun.) Maybe the fact that my Instagram account consists primarily of pictures of these cats—or the fact that I have an Instagram account at all—is infuriating to you. Maybe you think this proves the point that I'm a "cupcake-eating cheerleader," and not a "serious" professional woman. I think a "serious" woman can also be a crazy cat lady, and I will be rescuing cats until someone has to rescue me.

Politics, Now with Less Navy

A few days ago, for the first time in a long time, I had no choice but to go to J.Crew. I'd been reading up on Wendy Long, a staunchly conservative Christian politician from New York, and it was clear my post–White House wardrobe of Birkenstocks and patterned linen dresses was not going to help me in my quest to impersonate her. I needed navy, and lots of it.

I was not playing dress-up for the purposes of some obscure, political Halloween party, where everyone is instructed to go as a candidate from the opposing party and you play pin the tail on the majority leader. I wasn't having an identity crisis or participating in an election-year cosplay convention. I wasn't trying to pull a weird prank on my coworkers by tricking them into thinking my autumn look was Republican Mom, nor was I engaged in a top secret bait-and-switch mission designed to befuddle and take down the New York GOP. No—I had been called to serve.

░ ░ ░

I've known Chuck Schumer, the incumbent New York senator who ran against Long in the 2016 election, for many years.

We met when I was working for Obama in the Senate, and we worked together a lot during the 2006 midterms—Schumer was the chair of the Democratic Senatorial Campaign Committee, and Obama was traveling so much on behalf of candidates that year. In many ways, Long was running a kamikaze campaign against him; in such a liberal state, she had little chance of taking the Senate seat he's held for 18 years, and she'd already lost to one sitting New York senator, Kirsten Gillibrand, in 2012. The New York Republicans picked her as Schumer's opponent because she was the only person willing to do it.

But even if you're a shoo-in for something, you should always come prepared. About four weeks before the election, I got an email from Chuck Schumer's office asking if I would be interested in playing Long in the mock debates he'd use to get ready to face the wall of her conservative proposals. I thought it would be fun, so I said sure.

I'd been in the room during debate prep before, but not as the challenger. I never jumped in during Obama's sessions; the closest I came to the action was when I had to go to Neiman Marcus and buy 10 different red ties for John Kerry to test on camera—we had to see which one "burned hot." So I dove into my own preparations head-on.

Chuck's chief of staff, Mike Lynch, instructed me to keep my assignment top secret—I wasn't even supposed to tell David, though I already had before they told me not to—and the team sent me a packet of materials to bone up on Long's positions and style. They also sent me a list of questions a moderator might ask her—without the answers, so I could come up with them myself.

I had no idea how into it I'd get. I printed out five different types of documents, organized them in a binder, and wrote out my own glossary and index of questions. I watched videos of past debates to get her reactions down; I studied lists of remarks she'd made about various issues—health care, ISIS, gun control—and went over background research that I could use to support her views. I started off each day by reading her campaign's press releases. After I noticed she seemed to do a fair amount of tweeting herself (you can always tell), I followed her on Twitter, and then I read her entire feed. I developed a deep understanding of her evolution from relatively subdued and respectful Christian conservative to full-on Donald Trump supporter, complete with effusive praise for Hero Julian Assange and an absolutist stance on the Second Amendment. She still doesn't swear, though.

To top it all off, I analyzed her look. Chuck's team told me I should "just wear an outfit from the White House," but I got rid of all those clothes when I left—there was no way I was going to show up to work at VICE in an A-line skirt and a blazer, and I had no desire to. But at J.Crew, I went full on Professional Woman: navy blazer, navy pants, navy T-shirt. I paired that with navy shoes I had in my closet and the pearls I bought when I went to China with POTUS. The day of the debate, I even did my hair with rollers. (Wendy likes a lot of volume.)

When I came out of the bathroom, the worst possible thing happened: David exclaimed, "Oh, you look so nice!"

I met Mike and Lindsay Kryzak, Schumer's head of digital, for a wholesome, Christian meal of chicken and gravy, washed it down with a bourbon on the rocks, and walked into the New School's Tishman Auditorium ready to advance a hard line on immigration, binder in hand.

I felt reasonably confident on my grasp of Wendy's positions—one aspect of her stance on gun control even made me a little sympathetic, for a second—but I was kind of nervous about my delivery. There were about 30 people in the audience, and I didn't want to blow it—if Chuck somehow bombed his actual debate, it could have lasting consequences. He was in line to become either the majority or minority leader of the Senate.

We weren't allowed to interact before, but I could tell Chuck was pleasantly surprised when they introduced Wendy and she turned out to be me—the last time we'd seen each other, David and I had met him and his wife for dinner in Williamsburg.

But if he thought I was going to go easy on him, he was mistaken. We approached each other and shook hands.

"Nice to meet you, Ms. Long," Chuck said.

"Actually," I replied, "it's Mrs."

"Oh, so that's how it's going to be."

We were off. Chuck did great, but I held my own, even getting a little sanctimonious when the time was right. It was fun and creative—I said "Make America great again" at least three times, and I cracked a smile for only one of them. (Soon it wouldn't be funny anymore, but at the time everyone else laughed, too.)

While we weren't allowed to talk beforehand, I was too excited not to say anything to Chuck afterward. "That was so fun!" I told him as we shook hands for the second time. "Do you think I could be an actress?"

Chuck paused for a moment before replying. "No."

* * *

When I left the White House, I was so worried: that I would never see my friends again, that I would never be successful on my own, that I had given up the one thing that made me who I was. But as I adjusted, sometimes painfully, to my new life, I realized both that I could live without it and that it would never really go away—not least because politics affects most, if not all, aspects of our lives.

Now, my involvement has become less about me and more about what I can do. I'm not talking about what I can "contribute"; I'm talking about how I can be a real, invested part of the country. In the days after the 2016 election, several former Obama staffers expressed the sense that, after they left the White House, they had believed they could just kind of fade away into the background of the political sphere, popping up as a surprise debate practice partner or podcast guest when it was convenient or fun. The results made it clear this was not the case: We will have to be active, resourceful leaders of a new movement. I am not a political beast; I don't need to be working on campaigns or cycling through administrations all the time. But I can do a lot, and I know that I have to. Besides, if I'm being completely, totally honest, there are a couple of (female) politicians out there whose work I really, really believe in. If any of those women ever decided to make a big run for it, and if they thought I could serve them well, I would have a very hard time saying no.

While many people are disillusioned with our government and the political system that enables it, I just cannot think that way—even when it's too frustrating, or upsetting, or terrifying to watch. Although I have no idea what will happen next, I do know that it would be a denial of everything I learned working for Barack Obama to give up or opt out. Politics will always be a twinkle in my eye—the thing that makes me say "What if?"

Acknowledgments

If it weren't for my parents, I would have dedicated this book to Possum and Plouffe. A part of me regrets giving up the opportunity to make them very uncomfortable by doing so. I can't thank them enough for all they've taught me.

I would also like to thank:

- Cara Schembri, for being the best friend, mom, and feminist I know;
- Danielle (Dey) Crutchfield, Jess Wright, and the rest of Team SkedAdv, for always saying yes and proving that family comes in all different packages. I hope this book begins to honor your work and commitment;
- Amy Volpe, for enduring early-twenties me as a roommate, for making me live up to my potential, and for always bringing me back to reality when necessary;
- The rest of the women who show me how to be: Lea Goldman, Mindy Kaling, Amanda de Cadenet, Sophia Amoruso, Chelsea Handler, Jennifer Justice, Penny Pritzker, Nancy Dubuc, Audrey Gelman, Annie Karni,

Hildy Kuryk, Jennifer Gonring, Rachel (and Rubes) Sklar, Amie Parnes, Julie Frederickson, Janet Mock, Kirsten Gillibrand, Kate Bernstein, Jocelyn Leavitt, Rachel Shechtman, Alex and Vanessa Kerry, Amel Monsur, Ciel Hunter, Kim Kelly, Elisa Bluming, Cathy Simmons, Kate Fleck, Lauren Frankle, Anne Finucane, Lisa Halliday, and Helen Brosnan;

- Little Axe Salon, for filling my life with good hair days;
- Dr. Bonn, Doc Jackson, and Dr. Goldberg, for giving my gastrointestinal and gynecological stories happy endings. Additional praise goes to Tampon Queen Molly Hayward for making Cora a reality. Lauren Talarico also deserves a medical shout-out for being the only veterinary neurosurgeon I'd trust any cat I love with (and for making me a god-mommy);
- Brat, Megara, Sam, Jill, Grodi, and Fogel, for loving me despite the fact that I was in college and kind of a mess;
- Nancy Ashbrooke and Alex Detrick, for welcoming me at VICE;
- Michael Smith, for making sure my hair wasn't too puffy for *Charlie Rose* and for taking care of me after I left the White House;
- Tina Tchen and Valerie Jarrett, for showing me how to be a woman at the White House;
- Kathy Ruemmler and Peaches DeParle, for being like sisters;
- Julianna Smoot, Anne Olaimey, and Stephanie Cutter, for looking out for me when I didn't know how;

- Reggie Love, for teaching me why people should play team sports;
- Charlie Rose, Maneesh Goyal, and Samantha Jacobson, for showing me that I don't always have to be behind the scenes;
- Melissa Winter, Laurie Rubiner, Lona Valmoro, and Tovah Ravitz-Meehan, for taking me in;
- Joe Paulsen, Bobby Schmuck, and Eugene Kang, for knowing exactly what I needed, when I needed it;
- Anita Decker Breckenridge, for winking at me when no one else would;
- Clay Dumas and Dan Brundage, for supporting me in every way possible throughout my time in the White House and after, and for not being judgmental when I lost my shit over fucked-up grilled cheese sandwiches;
- Jon Favreau, for always being there (and down for Ruby Tuesday);
- Robert Gibbs, for being my ally, and for getting Bruce Springsteen to call me;
- Marv Nicholson, for teaching me to enjoy the simple things in life, like predicting the temperature and to always be kind;
- Dan Pfeiffer, for his encouragement, friendship, and trust, without which I would not be the person I am today (I would also be much worse at Twitter);
- Ferial Govashiri, for her bottomless generosity, for thinking I had style, and for speaking Farsi to Shrummie;

- Deb Futter, Sean Desmond, and Rachel Kambury at Twelve, for never giving up on me (even if they probably wanted to);
- Lauren Oyler, for helping make this book happen (and for being one of the smartest people I will ever know);
- Pete Souza, for the memories and for letting us print some of them here;
- Joe Biden, for being, as the memes suggest, one of the best dudes out there;
- Barack and Michelle Obama, for everything;
- David, for being the best guy who always puts us first;
- Petey and BunBun, for only sometimes peeing in the shower;
- And Shrummie.